SETTING OUR SIGHTS
ON HEAVEN

SETTING OUR SIGHTS
ON
HEAVEN

Why It's Hard
And Why It's Worth It

Paul D. Wolfe

THE BANNER OF TRUTH TRUST

THE BANNER OF TRUTH TRUST
3 Murrayfield Road, Edinburgh EH12 6EL, UK
P.O. Box 621, Carlisle, PA 17013, USA

*

© Paul D. Wolfe 2011

ISBN: 978 1 84871 143 3

*

Typeset in 11/15 Adobe Caslon Pro at
The Banner of Truth Trust, Edinburgh

Printed in the USA by
Versa Press, Inc.,
East Peoria, IL

To the saints of
New Hope Presbyterian Church
in Fairfax, Virginia,
with whom I share the privilege of
going to heaven every Sunday morning
at 9:30.

Contents

Foreword

IF you have picked up and opened this book because you are intrigued by the title and wonder what Paul Wolfe's 'take' on heaven might be, I would like to make a suggestion.

By all means read *Setting Our Sights on Heaven*. You will find it enormously helpful. But first, if you have not already done so, buy and read an earlier book by Paul Wolfe, because it will help you understand why he wrote this one. And it will also reassure you that he has walked along the pathway he describes in these pages.

That earlier book is entitled *My God is True!*[1] But it is the subtitle that will arrest your attention: *Lessons Learned Along Cancer's Dark Road*. It tells the story of a very significant part of his personal pilgrimage. This later book is not so much a continuation of that story as it is a chronicling of the meditations of the author on the gospel lifestyle that brightens every road.

Books on heaven, its nature and inhabitants, constitute a minor industry in contemporary publishing. Near-death experiences, after-death experiences, visiting-heaven-and-returning-to-earth experiences, all regularly emerge from the press and feed the peculiar fascination of our society (and sometimes our churches) with heaven.

It is rare, however, to find a book like this one. And, truth to tell, many books of this genre fail to produce in their readers what

---

[1] Paul Wolfe, *My God is True! Lessons Learned Along Cancer's Dark Road* (Edinburgh: Banner of Truth, 2009).

a true sense of heaven always does—a heavenly-mindedness that pervades the whole of life, fills the heart with love for Christ, and transforms a person's character as they set their sights on heaven.

It is still often said today that some people are 'too heavenly-minded to be any earthly use'. But gospel-centred thinking reverses that naïve adage. As C. S. Lewis once eloquently put it:

> If you read history you will find that the Christians who did most for the present world were just those who thought most of the next. The Apostles themselves, who set on foot the conversion of the Roman Empire, the great men who built up the Middle Ages, the English Evangelicals who abolished the Slave Trade, all left their mark on Earth, precisely because their minds were occupied with Heaven. It is since Christians have largely ceased to think of the other world that they have become so ineffective in this. Aim at heaven and you will get earth 'thrown in'; aim at earth and you will get neither.[2]

Paul Wolfe has learned this in a personal way. It is clear that in the process he has become deeply acquainted with the teaching of God's Word. He has also sat at the feet of some of the great masters of the spiritual life. He has tested his own thinking and digested their wisdom, and this has ensured that his own thinking is free from personal eccentricities, speculations, or hobby-horses that could divert us from a God-honouring view of heaven, a Christ-centred perspective on it, and a Spirit-given heavenly-mindedness in the present world.

More than that, *Setting Our Sights on Heaven* will take beginners by the hand and gently lead them on, but at the same time will refresh and reinvigorate more mature believers. It is biblical, and full of helpful meditation. It is practical and has a ring of both

---

[2] C. S. Lewis, *Mere Christianity* (1952), *The Complete C. S. Lewis Signature Classics* (San Francisco: Harper, 2002), p. 75.

truth and life. It is wonderfully simple in the best sense, clear and fresh like the water of a mountain stream.

In many places in the English-speaking world today, public buildings and hotels have become 'smoke-free' zones. Before, the air might be filled with smoke but only the most sensitive found it distressing. Now, however, in a smoke-free environment, it takes only one person who has been smoking to enter an elevator for everyone to become conscious that the atmosphere has been changed. Spiritually, however, the reverse has taken place. We live in such an earth-bound and spiritually polluted atmosphere that hardly anyone notices. We have become insensitive to the smoke; this-world-focused, self-absorbed lives are regarded as normal. We are inexperienced in breathing in heavenly air. But the soul that has breathed in heaven's joyful passion for the glory of God senses more and more just how abnormal, fallen, and distorted this-world-focused life has become.

The heavenly-mindedness to which Paul Wolfe introduces us brings us into a realm of grace and purity even while we live in this world. Breathing in that atmosphere produces attractive as well as holy lives. And from the earliest pages of *Setting Our Sights on Heaven*, you will be able to tell the difference! As the subtitle wisely suggests, this may be 'hard', but it is certainly '. . . worth it'.

So, read on, and join Paul Wolfe in setting your sights on heaven!

SINCLAIR B. FERGUSON
The First Presbyterian Church
Columbia, South Carolina
USA

Acknowledgments

I am an Associate Pastor. Look over the staff directories of some congregations and you will find Associate Pastors for Outreach and Evangelism, Associate Pastors for Small Group Ministries, Associate Pastors for Worship and Music, Associate Pastors for Youth Ministries, and so forth. Sometimes I fear I run the risk of becoming an Associate Pastor for Telling Anecdotes about My Own Wonderful Children. That seems to be my niche.

You will find several such anecdotes in the pages that follow. As every father knows, sometimes children say things, or cause us to say things, that impress upon us deep truths in surprising ways. That has certainly been my experience as father to Henry, Philip and Charlotte. Perhaps I cannot 'acknowledge' their contributions in the same way I express appreciation for the help that others have provided. It would seem strange to thank my six- and five-year-olds for making this book possible. But the fact remains that God has used them to teach me about heaven, and I hope by this book to pass on something of what he has taught me. I pray that, years from now, Lord willing, my children will read this book, not groaning at the stories their father told about them without their permission, but grateful to discover that they were the unwitting instruments of God's work during their earliest days. In my life, that is surely what they have been.

Thanks are due to Sinclair Ferguson. For the second time in two years he listened patiently as I described a book I had in mind, and for the second time he said, 'Go for it' (or words to that effect). Well, I went for it, and here we are. I pray this book turns out to be the blessing to others that he and I both wanted it to be.

I am humbled that the Banner of Truth has been willing to publish this work (and my first one too), allowing me to put into print truths and experiences I have become eager to share. I would like to thank all the Banner staff, both in Edinburgh and in Carlisle, Pennsylvania, for the great work they do.

I also want to say a word about my father-in-law, Harold Olson. On the very day when I wrote about John Bunyan's *The Pilgrim's Progress* for the last chapter of this book, Hal died in the Lord, succumbing to cancer at the age of sixty-eight. It was sorrowful (because we had lost him), it was joyful (because he had gained heaven), but it was also remarkable, the convergence of my writing and his homecoming. You see, since the publication of *The Pilgrim's Progress* in 1678, few people have imbibed that book the way my father-in-law did. He read it over and over. That led to a wide-ranging interest in Bunyan's life and labours. He read Bunyan's other works, as well as works by others about Bunyan's works. He read books about Bunyan's life. He read books about Bunyan's England. He watched Bunyan-themed videos. He hung Bunyan-related artwork. He bought nearly every edition and version of *The Pilgrim's Progress* he came across, including a comic book version. (Yes, there is a comic book version. I know this because he gave me a copy as a gift. It is described as 'a modern adaptation' of Bunyan's work. Modern, it most certainly is.) He even took my mother-in-law on a Bunyan pilgrimage: they travelled to England and visited various sites that were significant in Bunyan's life. In all these ways he made himself into an amateur Bunyan scholar. Wonderfully, in studying *The Pilgrim's Progress* he was also studying heaven and how to get there. He had already learned the way to heaven and was faithfully following it, but I have no doubt Bunyan encouraged him to keep going, and to do so hopefully. Now his hopes have been realized. On the same day I was reading and writing about Emmanuel's Land and the Celestial City, he passed from the one to the other. I can't help but wonder if he and Bunyan have met. 'Hello, my name's Hal Olson. I read your book.' Perhaps Bunyan replied, 'Yes, I know. I met Linda. She tells me you took her to England.'

Finally, I want to acknowledge my wife Christy, who has proven patient and encouraging yet again. Several years ago I was told that the process of writing a book and seeing it through to publication is the closest a man can come to the experience of having a baby. Christy has brought three children into the world. This is now the second book I have written. If I write one more, will that make us even? No, she has done far more, and given far more, than I ever will. Best of all, she is my fellow heir of the grace of life.

PAUL D. WOLFE
June 2011
Fairfax, Virginia
USA

Introduction

WE have all had the experience of being stunned by words that someone else has just spoken. A surprising announcement at the family dinner table, perhaps, or an inappropriate revelation made around the office water cooler. With the words still hanging in the air and ringing in our ears, we were left wondering, 'Did he really just say that?' But have you ever been in the position of being stunned by something you just heard *yourself* say? I mean, stunned not because you had said anything terribly brilliant or shocking, but simply because your own words sunk in and confronted you with reality in a way you had not anticipated. I have, and I want to share the story.

Our children (now aged six and five) once went through a phase in which they regularly asked my wife and me to tell them what year it would be when they turned a certain age. This combined their fascinations with numbers and with growing up. 'Daddy, what year will it be when I'm 10?' 'Mommy, what year will it be when I'm 16?' 'Daddy, what year will it be when I'm 50?' And so on, and so on, and so on. (And then so on some more. Little children harbour no hesitancies about repetition.)

One day as we were driving home from an outing, one of our sons piped up from the back seat, picking up that well-worn theme. 'Daddy', he asked, 'what year will it be when I'm 80?' The multiple of ten made the math problem easy for even this liberal arts major to solve. '2084', I answered. And then I added, half to myself, 'Of course, by then your Mommy and I will be in heaven.'

And that's when I was stunned.

By then your Mommy and I will be in heaven.

Did I really just say that?

Admittedly this was no brilliant observation about God and man, no profound insight into the nature of time and eternity. It took no sophisticated training, not in mathematics, nor in biology, nor in theology, to reach the conclusion I had articulated. And yet the sound of those words—better, the *meaning* of them—floored me. It would be an exaggeration to say that I nearly drove off the road . . . but not much.

What was it, precisely, that I found so striking about that statement? It was, I believe, the sheer matter-of-fact-ness of it. It rolled off my tongue as easily as something like, 'This time next week we'll be in Pittsburgh visiting your Grandma and Grandpa Wolfe.' There was something about my brief aside that powerfully impressed upon me the reality of heaven and of my own heavenly destiny. There I was, thinking about a date certain on the calendar, and doing the math, and realizing that by the time that year rolled around I would be in the very presence of Jesus Christ.

There is so much *un*-certainty that surrounds the subject of heaven: What is that place like? What does Jesus look like? When precisely will I arrive there? And what will it be like in death to go there? In the midst of all that uncertainty, it was jarring to hear myself speak with certainty about a time to come, identifiable on the calendar, when I will no longer be here but there, seeing Jesus and sharing fellowship with countless souls who arrived there before me. It is one thing to say, '*Someday* I'll be in heaven.' I have sometimes spoken in such indefinite terms, and there is nothing wrong with doing so. But that day in the car I realized there was something surprisingly solid—surprisingly real—about fixing upon a specific future year and realizing that by then I will have crossed the River.

By the way, in case you're curious, Christy and I were both born in 1971, meaning that we will be 113 years old in the year 2084. It is exceedingly unlikely that we will not be in heaven by then. If it turns out that I do live that long here on earth, look me up and I will give you a free copy of this book.

LIFT THINE EYES

My experience in the car that day—the words I said, followed by the inward reaction they provoked—raised for me once again the issue of heavenly-mindedness. I found myself challenged again to consider questions like these: Do I grasp firmly that heaven is a real place? Do I believe assuredly that heaven is where I am going? More fully, do I believe that one day heaven is coming here (that is, when our heavenly Saviour, Jesus Christ, comes back here to renew this world)? And am I living day-to-day in the bright light of those realities?

The Bible itself raises this issue. The Apostle Paul urged the Christians in Colossæ to 'seek the things that are above, where Christ is, seated at the right hand of God. Set your minds on things that are above, not on things that are on earth' (*Col.* 3:1-2). The Apostle Peter urged Christians scattered throughout Asia Minor to 'set your hope fully on the grace that will be brought to you at the revelation of Jesus Christ' (*1 Pet.* 1:13). Notice that each apostle in his own way charged his readers to 'set' themselves on heaven. Paul did so by pointing them upward, to that world above. Peter did so by pointing them forward, to the Day when that world will be all in all. In each case the summons was essentially the same: borrowing words sung beautifully in Mendelssohn's *Elijah*, we can say that Paul and Peter urged their readers to 'Lift thine eyes.'

Of course, the apostles' words to those churches, we rightly receive as the words of our Saviour to us today. The calling remains unchanged: Christians in this age, as in every age, are meant to be a heavenly-minded, heavenly-hearted people.

So . . . why aren't we? To some degree every Christian struggles to live mindful of heaven, and sadly some Christians live as though they were entirely oblivious to it. Why do we find it so hard to live steadfastly heaven-directed, heaven-saturated lives?

This is a question I have mulled over in recent years. And I have done so not because the matter struck me as interesting to consider in the abstract. No, for me this has been personal. I have pondered this question precisely because I struggle to heed the summons that Paul and Peter set before us, the calling to live as a heaven-oriented man.

The pages that follow represent the fruit of those personal reflections. At least, I pray they will prove fruitful for those who read them! This book divides into two parts. In Part 1 we will consider the Bible's teaching about heaven and heavenly-mindedness, including the impact these truths ought to have in specific areas of our lives (for example, marriage and finances). In Part 2 we will turn our attention to the work of spiritual diagnosis and prescription: What are the various factors (personal and social, theological and moral, subtle and overt) that tend to push heaven out of our minds, and what can we do to push it back to where it belongs? What remedies does the gospel itself prescribe to restore our heavenly bearings?

Some suspect that immersing ourselves in the truths of heaven will only render us inattentive to the things of earth, even neglectful of vital relationships and responsibilities. But those who have tasted and seen the goodness of real, biblical heavenly-mindedness know the opposite to be true: the one who faithfully contemplates things unseen and things yet to come finds new zeal for the glory of God and the cause of Christ here on earth. 'Lift thine eyes', and see for yourself.

Part 1:
The World to Come

What presumption it would have been, once, to have thought
or spoken of such a thing, if God had not spoken it before us!

RICHARD BAXTER
The Saints' Everlasting Rest

CHAPTER ONE

From Beginning to End

DON'T worry. The following is not a multiple choice exam, just a selection of statements to get us started:

A. 'And God said, "Let there be an expanse in the midst of the waters, and let it separate the waters from the waters." And God made the expanse and separated the waters that were under the expanse from the waters that were above the expanse. And it was so. And God called the expanse Heaven.'

B. 'Do not lay up for yourselves treasures on earth, where moth and rust destroy and where thieves break in and steal, but lay up for yourselves treasures in heaven.'

C. 'Heaven. I'm in heaven. And my heart beats so that I can hardly speak. And I seem to find the happiness I seek when we're out together dancing cheek to cheek.'

In order, those are the words of:

A. Moses (describing the original shaping of the created order in Genesis 1),

B. Jesus (urging heaven-directed priorities upon his disciples in Matthew 6), and

C. Irving Berlin (although credit is due to notables such as Fred Astaire, Ella Fitzgerald and Frank Sinatra for singing those words).

You probably noticed what those three statements have in common: each refers to 'heaven'. But notice the differences too. In Genesis 1 'heaven' means 'sky', but in Matthew 6 the term refers to

3

something else: that realm within the created order, presently distinct from the earth, and unseen to those who remain here, where God is most clearly revealed and thus most intimately known—a realm to which Christians look forward and in light of which they live. And in the lyrics of Irving Berlin, 'heaven' seems to be some undefined place of excellence and ecstasy—a place so wonderful, so thrilling, that it serves as a fitting metaphor for the experience of the most delightful of earthly pleasures.

This is a book about heaven 'B', Jesus' meaning in Matthew 6 (although we will see that there is more to be said about it than Jesus said just then). Of course, meteorology and astronomy are noble and valuable sciences, but this is not a book about the sky. And yes, dancing can be delightful, as can singing about it, but in this book we will not be considering some generic ideal world that helps us to sing about mere earthly delights, even the best ones. In these pages we will lift our gaze to that place the Scriptures reveal to us: a place where the sweetest fellowship with God and his people is enjoyed, a place where sin and sorrow and death do not exist, a place currently cut off from the earth, but one day to be a 'new heavens and a new earth in which righteousness dwells' (*2 Pet.* 3:13).

More precisely, then, how may we frame a biblical understanding of 'heaven'?

Before we dive in, a brief word about vocabulary is in order. You may have noticed that we Christians tend to use the one word 'heaven' in two different, but related, senses: sometimes we use it to refer to that realm as it exists at present (the world above); other times we use it to refer to the new world that Christ will inaugurate on the day of his return (the world to come). Still other times we use the word broadly, without distinguishing between the two. The Bible itself gives us grounds to speak in these ways. After all, heaven-at-present is called God's dwelling place (Moses prayed, 'Look down from your holy habitation, from heaven, and bless your people Israel'—*Deut.* 26:15), and the world to come is described in those same terms ('Behold, the dwelling place of God is with man. He will dwell with them, and they will be his people, and God himself will be with them as their God'—*Rev.* 21:3). This means that the world above and the world to come are essentially the same heavenly world in two successive phases: the one (present) is the future-in-waiting, the other (final) is the future-in-fullness. Remember that knowing God is what makes heaven heavenly: 'This is eternal life', said Jesus (and eternal life equals heavenly life), 'that they know you the only true God, and Jesus Christ whom you have sent' (*John* 17:3). In the world above, all know God, and the same will be true of the world to come, where we will know him even better. Thus we can say, 'Heaven is now. Heaven is coming.' We will consider these themes more fully in the pages that follow.

Now, turning our attention to the present, we can begin by affirming that heaven is indeed a place, although we need to steer clear of the notion that heaven could be located on one of our maps if we could just travel far enough to find it, and then make a map big enough to show it. Heaven is a place in the sense that it belongs to the created order, and yet it lies beyond the reach of our natural senses in this life. Though this is mysterious to us, heaven must be some sort of 'there'—a location, a destination—where creatures can go. How do we know this? We know this, first of all, because Jesus Christ, the God-man, forever clothed in a true human nature, body and soul, has gone there in that nature: 'For Christ has entered, not into holy places made with hands, which are copies of the true things, but into heaven itself, now to appear in the presence of God on our behalf' (*Heb.* 9:24). We know further that angels are there, and they are finite creatures: 'But concerning that day or that hour, no one knows, not even the angels in heaven, nor the Son, but only the Father' (*Mark* 13:32). We know further that the souls of departed believers are there, and they are finite too: 'you have come . . . to the assembly of the firstborn who are enrolled in heaven, and to God, the judge of all, and to the spirits of the righteous made perfect' (*Heb.* 12:22-23). In that place believers enjoy a knowledge of God that is closer and fuller than anything they ever experienced here on earth. And because Jesus is both God and man, he is both the object of that knowing, as well as the one who leads his brothers to know the Father (*Heb.* 2:11).

So, Jesus is there. Angels are there. The spirits of Christians who have passed through death are there.

Now let us consider the question: Is God there too? Is God in heaven? We have already noted that Jesus Christ, the incarnate Son of God, is there by virtue of his humanity, but is the Triune God there, apart from the reality of incarnation?

Of course, there is a sense in which God is everywhere in the created order. God himself poses the rhetorical questions, 'Can a man hide himself in secret places so that I cannot see him? declares the LORD. Do I not fill heaven and earth? declares the LORD' (*Jer.* 23:24). The Apostle Paul affirms that we creatures are positively enveloped by the divine presence: 'In him we live and move and have our being' (*Acts* 17:28). In every place God is present as Creator-Sustainer in relationship to his creation, and heaven is no exception. But the question remains: Is God 'specially' present in heaven? In other words, is he *there* in a way that he is not *here?*

Well, as we noted above in Deuteronomy 26:15 ('Look down from your holy habitation, from heaven'), the Bible itself refers to heaven as God's dwelling place. Consider also Psalm 33: 'The LORD looks down from heaven; he sees all the children of man; from where he sits enthroned he looks out on all the inhabitants of the earth' (verses 13-14). Consider also the words of Jesus, who taught his disciples to address God as 'Our Father in heaven' (*Matt.* 6:9). But of course we need to be clear about what such language means.

Heaven is not the dwelling place of God in the sense that he is localized or contained there. After all, God in his being transcends the very category of space, which belongs to the created order. Remember Solomon's confession when he dedicated the newly built temple: 'But will God indeed dwell on the earth? Behold, heaven and the highest heaven cannot contain you; how much less this house that I have built!' (*1 Kings* 8:27). So, how do we make sense of those passages that seem to put God 'in' heaven?

The traditional label for such language is 'anthropomorphic', from the Greek words meaning 'man' or 'human being' (*anthropos*) and 'form' (*morphe*). Anthropomorphic language describes the being and actions of God in human terms in order to facilitate our understanding. For example, God does not have physical eyes, and yet the Bible can speak of 'the eyes of the LORD' (*Gen.* 6:8) in order to communicate to us the idea of his attentive knowing. And God did not need to catch his breath after creating all things, and yet the Bible can speak of his being 'refreshed' on the seventh day (*Exod.* 31:17) in order to communicate to us the idea of his taking satisfaction in the works of his hands, the way a human worker kicks back and enjoys the fruit of his labours after a job well done.

To speak of heaven as God's 'holy habitation' and to say that he is 'in heaven' is to use anthropomorphic language. God is pictured as dwelling there—more fully, as *enthroned* there, in a glorious palace, fit for a king—and as welcoming us into his presence, in order to communicate to us: (1) the reality of his sovereign transcendence over the created order, and (2) the intimacy of the fellowship that the inhabitants of heaven enjoy with him. As royal Ruler and as loving Father, God 'lives' there . . . and the very use of quotation marks around 'lives' signals that we are using anthropomorphic language too!

The prophet Isaiah records for us a vision he was given that brings many of these themes together:

In the year that King Uzziah died I saw the Lord sitting upon a throne, high and lifted up; and the train of his robe filled the temple. Above him stood the seraphim. Each had six wings: with two he covered his face, and with two he covered his feet, and with two he flew. And one called to another and said: 'Holy, holy, holy is the LORD of hosts; the whole earth is full of his glory!' (*Isa.* 6:1–3).

Here we have an anthropomorphic vision, to be sure: God is pictured *as if* he possessed human form, so that sitting is possible, and *as if* he lived in heaven, enthroned there as king of the universe. These images help us to understand the infinite and invisible. But Isaiah also gives us a glimpse of things as they really are: that is, there really are angels in heaven, basking in the holiness of God and giving him unending praise. And in the subsequent verses Isaiah himself, exposed to the brilliance of divine holiness in a way that sinners on earth usually are not, learns the lesson firsthand that only those whose guilt is taken away and whose sin is atoned for can endure that brilliance and confidently offer themselves in the service of God.

IN THE BEGINNING

So far, in considering the Bible's teaching concerning heaven, we have trained our attention on that world as it presently exists. In an effort to broaden our theological horizons, let us now consider what we might call the 'history' of heaven. That is, from Genesis to Revelation, what does Scripture have to say about heaven in the unfolding purposes of God?

When we turn our attention to such considerations, minds are usually drawn toward the future. And this is perfectly understandable. After all, heaven is where Christians will be but have not yet arrived. In short, 'heaven' brings to mind 'yet to come'.

It may seem strange, then, that our consideration of this subject should begin not with the future but with the past, not with the end but with the beginning. Here let us heed the wise counsel of Maria, the future Mrs von Trapp: 'Let's start at the very beginning. A very good place to start.' Put in technical theological terms (and technical theological terms are valuable, if for no other purpose than to impress your friends at parties): to consider 'eschatology' (the way things will turn out, from the Greek *eschatos,* meaning 'last'), we must first turn our attention to 'protology' (the way things were originally, from the Greek *protos,* meaning 'first').

'In the beginning, God created the heavens and the earth' (*Gen.* 1:1), and then, Genesis 1 tells us, he went about the work of ordering and filling what he had created. At the high point of that work was the creation of man in the image of God, made for fellowship with God. And fellowship with him was something our un-fallen parents did enjoy: there was divine-human communication (God spoke to them), plus there were divine-human analogies (God made them and commanded them in such a way that their life and activity were to resemble his). Finally, at the end of Genesis 2 we are told that 'the man and his wife were both naked and were not ashamed' (*Gen.* 2:25). The picture painted for us is one, not only of intimacy between Adam and Eve, but also of unstained fellowship between them and their holy Creator. There was, in other words, a kind of 'heaven on earth' that prevailed before the fall. God made man and woman to enjoy communion with him, and they did.

Still, it is important for us to recognize that there was a measure of uncertainty that characterized the original situation: that is, uncertainty with respect to Adam and Eve's own moral future. Listen to God's instructions—and God's warning—in Genesis 2: 'And the Lord God commanded the man, saying, "You may surely eat of every tree of the garden, but of the tree of the knowledge of good and evil you shall not eat, for in the day that you eat of it you shall surely die'" (verses 16-17). The rest of the story (in particular, the fall of man into sin in Genesis 3) confirms for us that that warning was no mere hypothetical. Sin was a real possibility. In the beginning man was put on probation—that is, he was put under a test—and there was no guarantee that he would pass it.

The *Westminster Confession of Faith* puts it this way: God made the first humans 'endued with knowledge, righteousness, and true holiness, after his own image; having the law of God written in their hearts, and power to fulfil it: and yet under a possibility of transgressing, being left to the liberty of their own will, which was subject unto change' (*WCF* 4.2). Notice that language at the end: 'under a possibility of transgressing, being left to the liberty of their own will, which was subject unto change'. Genesis does not answer all the questions we might pose about that state of affairs (for example, *how* could their disposition change from one of holiness to one of rebellion?), but the eventual outcome confirmed it was possible: their will did change, and they fell. That tells us something about the pre-fall experience of our first parents: though made holy (how else could God have made them?), Adam and Eve were not assured they would remain holy, and therefore did not yet enjoy the full, final fellowship with their Maker that such assurance would afford. In short, there was something unsettled—and therefore, presumably, slightly *unsettling*—for man about his original condition. He knew God, but he also knew there was the possibility of falling from that knowledge as he originally enjoyed it because of falling into sin.

To fill out the picture, we should also consider the positive side of that situation. Yes, Adam knew there was something unsettled about his relationship to God, but he also must have known that if he passed the test of obedience to which God put him, life would not stay that way. Uncertainty and unsettledness would give way to confirmation and complete communion. The last barrier between

God and man would be torn down, and man would be exalted.

No, there is no explicit statement to that effect anywhere in Genesis 1 and 2. But the first man was no dolt. He must have possessed and exercised the capacity to deduce from all he knew to be true—in particular: God's goodness, plus the uncertainty of his own moral future, plus the longings he felt for full, stable fellowship with God—that there had to be something more, something higher, and that his transition into that 'more' hinged upon his passing the probation.

Here we can use the technical theological terms I dropped before—the ones that will impress our friends at parties: built into 'protology' was 'eschatology'. In other words, God made the world with the future in view: God viewed it, of course, but so did man. The tree of life in the Garden of Eden—signalling, apparently, the prospect of confirmed, as opposed to unsettled, life (*Gen.* 3:22; *Rev.* 2:7)—was, as it were, an arrow pointing upward that God planted in the ground, directing Adam's gaze from life as it was to a higher life that might be: not a life removed from this earth, lived at some previously unreached altitude, but an even fuller, more satisfying human life enjoyed right here, on this same earth. Put simply: *in the beginning was the end*. No, the end was not yet realized—after all, we are still talking about the beginning!—but it was intended in the mind of God and then presented to man as his glorious future prospect.

'But wait', you interject, 'it sounds like you're saying creation before the fall wasn't perfect.' Well, that depends upon what you mean by 'perfect'. If you mean 'It can't get any better than this', then, no, it *wasn't* perfect. It was perfect in the sense that there was no sin and misery, and in the sense that it fully suited God's purposes. But it was not God's purpose that the Creator-creature relationship should be from the very beginning all that it might be. The created order before the fall was 'very good' (*Gen.* 1:31), but from the vantage point of human experience it was not 'as good as it gets'. And that is precisely the way God designed it.

What does all this mean? It means that the original experience of the human race was not as heavenly as it is possible for humanity to enjoy. There was, as I said, a kind of 'heaven on earth' in the Garden of Eden—man knew God—but there was also the prospect of a heaven even higher. In the beginning, when life was probationary, there was already the prospect of life eternal.

GREAT EXPECTATIONS

Where did the story go from there? We know all too well. After Genesis 1 and 2 comes Genesis 3. After creation and commandment came transgression and curse. The serpent (elsewhere identified as the Devil, *Rev.* 12:9) led Eve to disobey, and then Eve led Adam to disobey. Thus the period of probation ended with 'Test Failed', and the prospect of eternal life was not realized. On the contrary, heaven on earth was exchanged for sin-misery-death on earth. After their sin God told Adam and Eve that it would be so (*Gen.* 3:16-19; plus 2:17), and then it was so. Read the rest of Genesis, and then the rest of the Bible, and then the rest of human history, and you will see quite clearly that it has been so. Fellowship with God in God's world gave way to alienation from God, discord among men, frustration in work, and maladies of mind and body, culminating in death.

The Bible would be relatively brief—and awfully discouraging too—if the story stopped there. Creation, fall, curse, end of story, end of heaven. Thankfully the Bible keeps going. In fact, even before we leave Genesis 3 we hear the sound of grace and hope: addressing the serpent, God says, 'I will put enmity between you and the woman, and between your offspring and her offspring; he shall bruise your head, and you shall bruise his heel' (*Gen.* 3:15). Yes, the serpent scored a victory in the Garden, but God promised in the very wake of that moral catastrophe that the serpent would find the tables turned before all was said and done. It will take the whole Bible to unpack that cryptic promise, but already God had put the world on notice that the Heaven Project had not been abandoned.

And yet the cryptic character of that Genesis 3:15 promise is telling: God did not make it immediately clear what the fulfilment of his heavenly purposes would require, or how long it would take him (that is, how long from man's perspective) to fulfil them. Rome wasn't built in a day . . . and neither was the new Jerusalem! (See *Rev.* 21:2.) Read the Old Testament from start to finish and what you hear is the sound of a gradual crescendo. The original post-fall promise is increasingly clarified as subsequent covenants are forged by God with Abraham, Isaac and Jacob, and later with Israel under Moses, and even later with David, Israel's king. And along the way, especially later in Old Testament history, God speaks by his servants the prophets, reminding Israel of those past covenants and pointing them forward to future glory.

By the time you reach the end of the book of the Prophet Malachi (that is, the end of the Old Testament), you have a much clearer understanding than you did in Genesis 3 concerning God's heavenly intentions. You have learned, for example, that God is determined to renew the world, and thus create a new world in which man's eschatological aspirations will finally be realized (*Isa.* 65:17-25). And you have discovered that that glorious new world is going to be populated with representatives of the nations, and not just with the physical descendants of Abraham (*Isa.* 2:2-3). And you have learned that one day a Servant of God will come and suffer for sins and thus tear down the barrier that would prevent the realization of those aspirations (*Isa.* 52-53). And finally—if you can imagine yourself there in the silent centuries after Malachi, standing at that point on the timeline of redemptive history—you have learned to keep waiting, because you know that in your day the long-expected Messenger has not yet appeared (*Mal.* 3:1-4). And so you wait, and watch, and all faithful children of Abraham wait and watch with you. How long, O Lord? How long until man is raised?

OUR HEAVENLY PIONEER

At this point, following centuries of waiting after Malachi's prophetic ministry ceased, you must be eager for some good news. Well, the Bible has good news to tell: in the fullness of time, the Servant-Messenger did appear. How dramatic are those early Gospel chapters, which record for us the dawning of the great divine visitation! 'Do not be afraid, Mary, for you have found favour with God. And behold, you will conceive in your womb and bear a son, and you shall call his name Jesus' (*Luke* 1:30-31). As Paul puts it, 'when the fullness of time had come, God sent forth his Son, born of woman, born under the law' (*Gal.* 4:4). The Son of God came into the world. Why did he come? The Bible has many answers to that question, many different ways of summing up the Son's mission. Here is one: his mission was to go to heaven and lead his people there too. Now let us unpack that statement, because there is more to it than first meets the eye.

Because the Son of God is God (*John* 1:1), it would be impossible for him as God to 'go' anywhere (heaven included) in the sense of moving spatially from place to place within the created order. After all, in his divinity he is not even bound by space to begin with. No, here we have in view the incarnate Son in his humanity. The Son of God could, and did, go to heaven as the God-man. He took to himself a true human nature, body and soul, born of a woman, born in Bethlehem, and then in that nature lived a true human life that culminated in his own exaltation. Listen to Paul: God has 'seated him [Jesus Christ] at his right hand in the heavenly places, far above all rule and authority and power and dominion, and above every name that is named, not only in this age but also in the one to come' (*Eph.* 1:20-21). Listen to the writer of Hebrews: in Christ we have a high priest 'who is seated at the right hand of the throne of the Majesty in heaven' (*Heb.* 8:1). This was the overarching trajectory of his initial incarnate experience: life on earth, followed by exaltation unto life in heaven.

And he has gone there in his resurrection body. In this respect Jesus was the pioneer. Jesus was the firstfruits (*1 Cor.* 15:20). He was the first fully to pass from this age into the age to come, from the protological (first) order into the eschatological (last) order. He led the way. Paul traces this out in 1 Corinthians 15:

> But it is not the spiritual that is first but the natural, and then the spiritual. The first man was from the earth, a man of dust; the second man is from heaven. As was the man of dust, so also are those who are of the dust, and as is the man of heaven, so also are those who are of heaven (verses 46-48).

Adam ('the first man'), made from the dust, not yet exalted, represents the first order. Jesus ('the second man'), exalted into heaven in his resurrection body, represents the last order. He has become 'the man of heaven'. As it is sometimes put, Jesus Christ made his way 'from dust to glory'.

But to chart the Son's trajectory in these broad terms still leaves us short of the gospel. We have made a good beginning, but we need to keep going. Incarnation, then earthly life, then heavenly exaltation—as staggering as those realities are to contemplate— would not have been enough to accomplish what he came to do. Remember, his mission was to go to heaven *and lead his people there too.* Jesus himself said so:

> For I have come down from heaven, not to do my own will but the will of him who sent me. And this is the will of him who

sent me, that I should lose nothing of all that he has given me, but raise it up on the last day. For this is the will of my Father, that everyone who looks on the Son and believes in him should have eternal life, and I will raise him up on the last day (*John* 6:38-40).

In other words, Christ came not merely to live and rise and reign, but to save. God's heaven was always meant to be a full heaven—that is, one populated with his chosen ones—and because his chosen ones are all sinners (Christ himself excepted, of course), ransom was required.

So yes, the Son's incarnate career consisted of earthly life followed by heavenly life, but earthly death—more fully, the making of atonement by that death—would have to take place in between. In a manner of speaking, his route to heaven would have to pass through hell: that is, through the hellish experience of bearing our guilt and enduring his Father's wrath in our place. On the cross that is exactly what he did. He died for our sins (*Gal.* 1:4). And then he was buried, and then he was raised, and then he was exalted: 'After making purification for sins, he sat down at the right hand of the Majesty on high' (*Heb.* 1:3).

When the writer of Hebrews puts it that way—Jesus 'sat down' at God's right hand (plenty of anthropomorphic language there!)—he is picturing Jesus' installation as God's universal ruler upon the completion of his death and resurrection. But that language should not be interpreted to mean that Jesus has nothing at all left to do, simply because he is done with dying and rising. Remember, the ultimate goal was a new world—that is, a glorious new *physical* world fashioned out of the old—inhabited by all those whom the Father chose 'before the ages began' (*2 Tim.* 1:9), clothed in their resurrection bodies, living and serving free from sin, rejoicing in all the just and gracious works of God. Consider the present state of affairs—look at the world, read the newspapers, look at your own life—and you will see just how much of a discrepancy remains between present reality and that ultimate goal. According to Paul, it's as if the ground we walk on is 'groaning' under the weight of that discrepancy (*Rom.* 8:19-22), and we are groaning with it (verse 23). Thus we can say, as the nineteenth-century Dutch theologian Herman Bavinck put it, 'In his state of exaltation there still remains much for Christ to do.'[1]

What work remains for him to do? First, there is his work throughout this age: drawing all his Father's chosen ones to faith in himself, building them up in holiness while they live, and welcoming them into his presence when they die. Second, there is his work at the end of the age: returning in glory, raising the dead, judging all men, and renewing the world. When the dust settles on that last day, the Son's mission will have been accomplished. Heaven will have been brought to earth. The place where God is most clearly revealed and most intimately known will no longer be some mysterious realm removed from earthly experience. It will be the whole world. Thus we sing:

> This is my Father's world:
> The battle is not done;
> Jesus who died shall be satisfied,
> And earth and heav'n be one.[2]

You see, Jesus' mission was 'to go to heaven and lead his people there too' (as I put it before), not by removing us from the earth into a condition of unending disembodiedness, but by bringing about the breathtaking glorification of the original created order, his people included, body and soul, and the earth included too. Think of the way a candidate for President or Prime Minister

---

[1] Herman Bavinck, *Reformed Dogmatics*, vol. 3 (Grand Rapids, Michigan: Baker, 2006), p. 568.

[2] 'This Is My Father's World.' Words by Maltbie D. Babcock.

makes his case to the electorate: 'Here's where I want to take our country', he says, 'and here's how I intend to get us there.' He is speaking metaphorically: he has in mind, not literal relocation, but a better life for the people *on* location. So too, Christ's ultimate mission is not to get his people out of this place, but to perfect this place and his people along with it. In short, Christ will lead us, ultimately not by leading us *away*, but by leading us *into:* having gone first into the future by his own resurrection, he will lead us into the glory for which this world was originally designed. That was his mission from the beginning, and he will not fail his Father.

Grasp this. The mission of Jesus was not merely to get us back to the way things were before the fall. Remember, that was a circumstance of testing and unsettledness. Pre-fall life was probationary life, not confirmed life. Jesus came not to get us back to life as it was, but to advance us to life as it might have become. Put another way, Jesus' mission was not merely to restore but to raise. Do you see how good the good news really is? In Christ we are not put back under probation and told, 'Try again and don't blow it this time.' Instead he ushers us into the full inheritance that passing the probation would have gained. By his own obedience—obedience to the point of death, even death on a cross (*Phil.* 2:8)—Christ has gained it for us.

Thus there is a ring of gospel truth in the words of Joni Mitchell: 'We've got to get ourselves back to the garden.' True: in the Garden of Eden we knew God, and in the gospel of Jesus we return to God. But it is just that—only a faint ring. First, when it comes to salvation, we lack the capacity to 'get ourselves' anywhere on our own. It must be God who does the getting! And second, where he gets us is not merely 'back to the garden'. The good news is so much better than the granting of a second chance, a Garden of Eden 'do-over' (for you golfers, a 'mulligan'). Instead of 'back to the garden', instead of *The Way We Were,* try *Back to the Future:* Christ brings us back to God, but he does so in such a way that the future envisioned by God from the beginning is finally realized, for Christ has done it all.

These are grand, stirring themes. Thus it should come as no surprise to find that some Christian theologians have been inspired to reach rhetorical heights when they have sought to summarize these truths. Consider, for example, the following sweeping synopsis of redemptive history from the *Systematic Theology* of nineteenth-century Presbyterian minister and theologian Robert Dabney. Do you doubt that books with 'Systematic Theology' in the title can contain thrilling, practically poetic passages? Doubt no more.[3] Read this excerpt. In fact, read it out loud in suitably dramatic tones and imagine you can hear music swelling as you make your way:

> This conclusion gives us a noble view of the immutability of God's purpose of grace, and the glory of His victory over sin and Satan. This planet was fashioned to be man's heritage; and part of it, at least, adorned with the beauties of paradise, for his home. Satan sought to mar the divine plan, by the seduction of our first parents. For long ages he has seemed to triumph, and has filled his usurped dominion with crime and misery. But his insolent invasion is not to be destined to obstruct the Almighty's beneficent design. The intrusion will be in vain. God's purpose shall be executed. Messiah will come and re-establish His throne in the midst of His scarred and ravaged realm; He will cleanse away every stain of sin and death, and make the earth bloom forever with more than its pristine splendour; so that the very plan

---

[3] The title of this work as it was originally published makes it sound even more daunting: *Syllabus and Notes of the Course of Systematic and Polemic Theology Taught in Union Theological Seminary, Virginia.* Clearly, titles then were not meant to grab as they are now.

which was initiated when 'the morning stars sang together and the sons of God shouted for joy', will stand to everlasting ages.[4]

See? Systematic theologies can sing! Satan the Intruder, his intrusion will have been in vain. God the Creator, he will gain the victory. The world he made, he will redeem. Satan sought to ruin, but Christ has come to rescue and raise. And in the end he will have done it. Christ will descend and raise the world. He will fill it with a glorious resurrected human race. Thus will this world, now so terribly tarnished, finally shine with unending brilliance. Mission accomplished. Heaven realized. Glory be to God!

[4] Robert L. Dabney, *Systematic Theology* (Edinburgh: Banner of Truth, 1996), p. 852.

CHAPTER TWO

Show Me the Way To Go Home

IN Chapter 1 we considered the history of heaven from beginning to end: God made the world with heaven in view, and
Christ's mission was (and remains) to make the original vision into
reality. Here in Chapter 2 we focus our attention on the experience
of those who belong to Christ. His mission can only be deemed
'mission accomplished' if he eventually gets us there. 'Because
Christ is a perfect Saviour, who brings not only the possibility but
also the actuality of salvation, He cannot and may not and will not
rest before those who are His own have been bought by His blood,
been renewed by His Spirit, and brought where He is, there to be
the spectators and sharers of His glory (*John* 14:3 and 17:24).'[1] 'And
if I go and prepare a place for you, I will come again and will take
you to myself, that where I am you may be also' (*John* 14:3). That
was his promise, and that was his prayer: 'Father, I desire that they
also, whom you have given me, may be with me where I am, to see
my glory that you have given me because you loved me before the
foundation of the world' (*John* 17:24).

If we pose the question (and yes, my children have posed it;
perhaps you know children who have posed it too), How will Jesus
get us to heaven?—the answer goes something like this: he will
get us there by (1) our effectual calling, (2) our dying, and (3) his
returning. Admittedly, this answer sounds somewhat less exciting

---

[1] Herman Bavinck, *Our Reasonable Faith* (Grand Rapids, Michigan: Baker,
1977), p. 553.

than the answer 'by motorcycle', which is what I suspect my children—especially my sons—are hoping to hear. But it is a biblical answer. And because it is biblical, the more you reflect upon it, the more you realize just how exciting it really is! Think of it: he will get us there—better yet, at the end of the age he will get heaven here—and even death itself will serve his purpose along the way. No doubt when we have arrived, we will testify that no earthly ride, no matter how fast, no matter how thrilling, could ever compare.

1. OUR EFFECTUAL CALLING

'What is effectual calling?' The *Westminster Shorter Catechism* answers: 'Effectual calling is the work of God's Spirit, whereby, convincing us of our sin and misery, enlightening our minds in the knowledge of Christ, and renewing our wills, he doth persuade and enable us to embrace Jesus Christ, freely offered to us in the gospel' (*WSC* 31). Put simply, the Spirit changes sinners' hearts so that they trust in Christ for salvation. Thus are they 'called' to Christ: not merely summoned, 'Come to him', but also changed in such a way that they heed that very summons.

The one who has been changed in this way—changed deeply so as to believe truly—has thereby become an already heavenly man, even while he remains on earth. This is true in many respects. Here are three: the Christian possesses a heavenly disposition, heavenly desires, and a heavenly justification.

a. The Christian possesses a heavenly disposition.

To be clear, by 'disposition' I do not mean 'personality' or 'demeanour'. The word can mean that, but here I mean something else. I have in view the Christian's basic attitude toward God. Let me explain.

Notice in the *Shorter Catechism* language we just considered that the Christian is one whose mind has been enlightened and whose will has been renewed. This is at the heart of what the Bible means by being born again. Jesus told Nicodemus that the new birth was necessary for admission into the kingdom of God (*John* 3:3), and the apostles reminded Christians that they had experienced that life-changing blessing (*1 Pet.* 1:3). Prior to the experience of renovating grace, the son of Adam is earthly, as opposed to heavenly, in the worst way: not merely living on earth (which is good), but belonging to this 'present evil age' (which is not good; *Gal.* 1:4). Jesus put it this way: to those who opposed him he said, 'You are from below; I am from above. You are of this world; I am not of this world' (*John* 8:23). Apart from the Spirit's renewing work the sinner remains dead in trespasses and sins (*Eph.* 2:1, 5): he is blind to spiritual realities (*1 Cor.* 2:14) and 'hostile to God' (*Rom.* 8:7), even a 'hater of God' (*Rom.* 1:30). Paul sums it up in these terms: 'They are darkened in their understanding, alienated from the life of God because of the ignorance that is in them, due to their hardness of heart' (*Eph.* 4:18). Yes, that is strong language, but it is the Bible's language, so we dare not tone it down.

Thankfully, the Spirit's work in effectual calling is to bring deadened sinners to life. His work takes place deep within—in fact, in the deepest recesses of the human heart. There he brings about a momentous change, a spiritual resurrection, wherein the sinner's heart is radically redirected. The end result is a man who, in terms of his fundamental orientation, is no longer anti-God but pro-God, no longer bent away from divine things but drawn to them, no longer resistant to the gospel but disposed to embrace it. In short, the Christian has been given a heavenly heart. In the world above, all love God, men and angels alike, and the Christian on earth, though not yet arrived in heaven, has spiritually joined them.

Now, here's the very good news: once renovated in this way, the believer will never become un-renovated. Once raised to new life, he will never find himself cast back down to where he was before. Jesus said, 'Whoever believes in the Son has eternal life' (*John* 3:36). How strange it would be if this eternal life turned out to be 'temporary eternal life' after all! Peter said, 'you have been born again, not of perishable seed but of imperishable, through the living and abiding word of God' (*1 Pet.* 1:23). Would the imperishable, abiding word of God be the instrument of granting a perishable, fleeting new birth? Listen again to Robert Dabney:

> It is a most low and unworthy estimate of the wisdom of the Holy Ghost and of His work in the heart, to suppose that He will begin the work now, and presently desert it; that the vital spark of heavenly birth is an *ignis fatuus*,[2] burning for a short season, and then expiring in utter darkness; that the spiritual life communicated in the new birth, is a sort of spasmodic or galvanic vitality, giving the outward appearance of life in the dead soul, and then dying.[3]

Thank God, the new life the Spirit grants is no such fleeting, dying flame. Once lit, it burns forever, for the Spirit sustains it. The believer is forever aflame with heavenly love.

Jonathan Edwards described the believer's new disposition in similar 'fiery' terms:

> This holy, heavenly spark is put into the soul in conversion, and God maintains it there. All the powers of hell cannot put it out, for God will keep it alive, and it shall prevail more and more. Though it be small, yet it is powerful; it has influence over the heart to govern it, and brings forth holy fruits in the life, and will not cease to prevail till it has consumed all the corruption that is left in the heart, and till it has turned the whole soul into a pure, holy, and heavenly flame, till the soul of man becomes

[2] A temporary, ghostly light.
[3] Dabney, *Systematic Theology*, p. 692.

like the angels, a flame of fire, and shines as the brightness of the firmament.[4]

Just think, Christian: such an eternal flame has begun to burn in you!

Of course, this does not mean the believer no longer sins. He does so regularly, and sometimes grievously. The Christian does not perfectly manifest in practice what is true of him in principle. In the deepest recesses of his heart he has been re-oriented toward God, and it shows in new obedience, but that deep-seated orientation exists beneath layers of sinful patterns and desires. This is precisely why he finds the Christian life to be a battle every day. Love for God is now his defining orientation—his internal moral compass now points heavenward—but the vestiges of sin remain. Thus the moral conflict to which Paul bears witness in Romans 7 ensues: 'For I do not do the good I want, but the evil I do not want is what I keep on doing' (*Rom.* 7:19). Still, the very reality of that daily battle is a good sign! It signifies that deep change has indeed taken place. Yes, the Christian sins, but as Paul puts it, there is a sense in which he does not want to sin, since there is a love for God that burns more deeply. And he looks forward to the day when that desire will burn most brightly, without any inward opposition to quench it, for the vestiges of sin will be no more. In heaven he will love the Lord his God with all his heart and with all his soul and with all his mind, holy and without blemish, and the battle will be done.

Here again we see that the gospel does more than get us back to the Garden. Though Adam was made holy, he could not be certain he would persevere in holiness, and eventually he fell. But the Christian does possess that certainty, for he has the divine promise of eternal preservation. In this respect the Christian is re-made in

[4] Jonathan Edwards, 'The Portion of the Righteous', in *The Works of Jonathan Edwards*, vol. 2 (Edinburgh: Banner of Truth, 1995), p. 888.

the image of God, shining with godlikeness even more brightly than Adam did at first. As we noted before from the *Westminster Confession of Faith*, man was originally made 'endued with knowledge, righteousness, and true holiness, after his [God's] own image'—in that respect he was like God—'and yet under a possibility of transgressing'—in that respect he was not like God. But the one who has been born again is under no possibility of transgressing in the sense of finally and fatally turning away from the truth. This is not because he is strong enough to preserve his own new nature, but because God is more than strong enough, and he will do it. Consider, this is to reflect the character of God. After all, God must delight in his own immutable holiness, and the Christian—like God's holy ones in heaven—can say, 'I delight in mine too!' God possesses immutable holiness as the original, and he is pleased by his promise and power to impart this to his children as a gift. Thus, in the deepest depths of the Christian's being, he has been raised—raised to love God—and God will never let him fall back down, not to where he was before that spiritual resurrection took place.

b. The Christian is animated by heavenly desires.

This follows from his new disposition. Because he now possesses a holy, heavenly love for God, the believer longs to see God given his due. And what is God's due? 'To him is due from angels and men, and every other creature, whatsoever worship, service, or obedience he is pleased to require of them' (*Westminster Confession of Faith* 2.2). The Christian says, 'Yes! May it be so. That's what I want to see.' Those in heaven long to see God praised, and the believer on earth does too. Those in heaven desire to see all God's chosen ones brought into the kingdom, and the Christian here does too. Those in heaven long to see God's justice vindicated, and the believer on earth shares that longing with them.

In the Psalms we see these new desires expressed in prayer. 'Be exalted, O God, above the heavens! Let your glory be over all the earth!' (*Psa.* 57:5). 'That your beloved ones may be delivered, give salvation by your right hand and answer us!' (*Psa.* 60:5). 'Arise, O God, defend your cause; remember how the foolish scoff at you all the day!' (*Psa.* 74:22). The words of Psalm 119 sound a similar tone:

> Oh that my ways may be steadfast in keeping your statutes! (verse 5).

> It is good for me that I was afflicted, that I might learn your statutes (verse 71).

> It is time for the LORD to act, for your law has been broken (verse 126).

> My eyes shed streams of tears, because people do not keep your law (verse 136).

Can you hear the new value system, the new priorities, emanating from those words in Psalm 119? We do not know who wrote that Psalm, but we certainly know what they deeply desired: they wanted to see God glorified in the keeping of his law, and thus they wanted to see God act powerfully and graciously to bring about that state of affairs. God's holy ones in heaven want to see the very same thing, although, unlike the Psalmists, they are no longer surrounded by sin—even plagued by their own sin—in such a way as to be driven to tears. Still, these are the priorities of heaven.

We see these same values reflected in the words of the Lord's Prayer, especially its opening petitions. Jesus taught his disciples to pray, 'Our Father in heaven, hallowed be your name. Your kingdom come, your will be done, on earth as it is in heaven' (*Matt.* 6:9–10). The Christian's response is not to complain, 'Oh Jesus, do I have to? Do I really have to pray those prayers?' No, he gladly makes such requests of his Father (whether he uses the precise words of

Matthew 6 or not). When his heart is properly oriented, he cannot not make them. He cries out. These petitions in the Lord's Prayer are not imposed upon reluctant Christians against their will, keeping them praying when they would 'rather be fishing' (to borrow from the bumper sticker). No, the Lord's Prayer gives expression to Christians' most ardent desires. And Jesus could only have taught us to pray this way if they were his desires too. They were, and they still are. These are the priorities of our heavenly King.

Here in the United States some are driven by what is known as 'the American Dream'. The one who dreams it pictures something like this: to be married with children, living in a nice house with a picket fence and an ample backyard in a safe neighbourhood, spending Monday-through-Friday daytime in satisfying labour, and then giving evenings and weekends to rejuvenating leisure . . . and preferably minimal yard work. Now there is much that is good about that dream. It reflects fundamental human desires, and it is proper for the Christian to seek the fulfilment of those desires. But he will do so with higher aspirations reigning in his heart and thus directing his life. His earthly pursuits will be governed by heavenly desires. Look him in the eye and ask him, 'What do you *really* want?' (and emphasize 'really' to make the point). His answer will not be: 'wife and children and picket fence'. His answer (to make use of *Westminster Shorter Catechism* Q. 1) will be: 'to glorify God and to enjoy him forever, and to live in a world where everyone around me does too'. This is the Christian Dream. Here on earth he may enjoy something approximating the American Dream, or he may not. (By the way, look around: most do not, especially if you lift your gaze and look around the whole world.) But whatever his earthly fortunes may be, it is his heavenly dream that truly drives him. And best of all—and those in heaven know this better than we do—this is a dream that will most certainly come true. Christian, do you want to glorify and enjoy God? Do you want to live in a world where everyone else does too? Guess what: the saints and angels in heaven feel the same way, and right now they are gazing upon the One who lived and died and lives again to make it happen. It will happen. 'Blessed are those who hunger and thirst for righteousness, for they shall be satisfied' (*Matt.* 5:6). After all, your Father in heaven and the Son at his right hand desire it far more earnestly than you do. Infinitely more. It will happen.

c. The Christian possesses a heavenly justification.

Protestant Christians have long recognized that the blessing known as 'justification' is of central importance in the experience of salvation. Paul accords it such significance in his letters to the Galatians and the Romans. Sadly, many Protestants today, if asked what justification means, would hem and haw with uncertainty like nervous students ill-prepared for a vital test question. Away with such uncertainty. Let's get this one straight!

The *Westminster Shorter Catechism* sums it up this way: 'Justification is an act of God's free grace wherein he pardoneth all our sins and accepteth us as righteous in his sight, only for the righteousness of Christ imputed to us, and received by faith alone' (*WSC* Q. 33). In other words, justification refers to that crucial saving blessing, granted the believer upon his coming to faith, in which God the Judge, presiding in his heavenly courtroom, pronounces the sinner entirely forgiven of all crimes and perfectly acceptable according to the requirements of the law. In short, God now views the man as having perfectly obeyed him, and says so. Of course, God views the sinner that way not because the sinner did perfectly obey him. After all, he is a sinner! No, God sees him as righteous because he sees him clothed with the very righteousness of Jesus Christ, whose life was one of spotless obedience from beginning to end. By faith alone the believer is so united with Christ as to be regarded by God as having obeyed as faithfully as Christ, and thus entitled to the inheritance that belongs to those who have done so. Connect this to creation: when God made man he put him under probation, testing his obedience in the Garden of Eden, and man failed; in justification the sinner, brought before the divine Judge, hears the wonderful verdict, 'Probation passed! Enter into your reward.' If anyone in the courtroom objects, 'But your Honour, he *didn't* pass! Look at his record. Look at his crimes', the Judge responds, 'I will entertain no such accusations. Another has passed the probation in his stead, and I regard the standing of that faithful one as belonging to the man before me.' Verdict rendered. Case closed. And what a wonderful closing! As J. I. Packer puts it, 'Justification is forgiveness *plus;* it signifies not only a washing out of the past, but also acceptance and the gift of a righteous man's status for the future.'⁵

Where does the Bible teach this? Among other places it teaches this at the climax of 2 Corinthians 5: Paul writes, 'For our sake he made him to be sin who knew no sin, so that in him we might become the righteousness of God' (verse 21). Paul does not use the word 'justification' in that verse, but the concept is plainly present. There Paul speaks of Jesus and of his atoning work, and then of the blessing that belongs to us as a result. On both sides of the gospel transaction (Christ's side and ours) judicial realities are in view. Of course Jesus was not 'made sin' in the sense of becoming a sinner. Notice, 'he knew no sin'. Rather, on the cross Jesus took the guilt of our sin upon his shoulders and suffered God's just judgment accordingly. So too, the believer does not 'become the righteousness of God' in the sense of being made perfectly righteous immediately—the believer remains a sinner—but in the sense of gaining the status of 'righteous' before the law and Lawgiver. Our sin was imputed (that is, credited, or charged) to Christ on the cross, and his righteousness is now imputed to us. What a glorious exchange!

⁵ J. I. Packer, *I Want to Be a Christian* (Wheaton, Illinois: Tyndale, 1977), p. 91.

Teaching the Roman Christians about justification, Paul cites this Davidic beatitude: 'Blessed are those whose lawless deeds are forgiven, and whose sins are covered; blessed is the man against whom the Lord will not count his sin' (*Rom.* 4:7-8; *Psa.* 32:1-2).

How is justification a heavenly blessing? In three ways.

First, to be justified is to possess the same right to heaven that belongs to those who are already there. The world above is presently populated with justified believers. Everyone in heaven has a right to be there because they are clothed with the righteousness of Christ which entitles them to share in his reward. We believers on earth possess the same righteous status, and thus the same heavenly right. We have not yet gained admission, as they have, but we are no less entitled. As those plagued by lingering doubts and discouragement, we sometimes struggle to grasp that this is true—some struggle mightily—but it is true. Christians on earth are no less justified than those in heaven.

> More happy, but not more secure,
> The glorified spirits in heav'n.[6]

'Who shall bring any charge against God's elect? It is God who justifies' (*Rom.* 8:33). Once God justifies a man, the divine verdict shall never be overturned. We shall certainly be accepted into the world above, because we have already been declared acceptable by God himself.

Second, justification is heavenly in that it anticipates the day when the believer will go to heaven through death. When a man dies 'the dust returns to the earth as it was, and the spirit returns to God who gave it' (*Eccles.* 12:7). In other words, as it is often put, in death a man 'goes to meet his Maker'. But for the believer that meeting will be no dreadful occasion, for he will hear the Judge of all the earth, now his heavenly Father, pronounce him, 'Forgiven.

---

[6] 'A Debtor to Mercy Alone.' Words by Augustus Toplady.

Righteous. Welcome!' What he long believed to be true will be newly and powerfully reinforced for him, and he will rejoice with joy immeasurable.

Third, justification is heavenly in that it anticipates the day when the new world—Christ's heavenly world—will be fully ushered in. On the last day, when Jesus returns in glory and judges every man, those who believed in him 'shall be openly acknowledged and acquitted in the day of judgment' (*Westminster Shorter Catechism* Q. 38). On that day believers will not become more justified than they were before, for they were fully pronounced forgiven and righteous when they first came to Christ. Thus no increase is possible. But the verdict of their justification will be made public as never before, declared loudly and clearly for all to hear, believers and unbelievers alike, angels and demons too. It must be so. After all, God's name must be vindicated. In the end he must be recognized by all as the just Judge he has always been. And for that to happen all must be eye-and-ear witnesses to the righteousness of his judicial dealings, including the justifying of his elect. This helps us to appreciate the significance of our justification in the present. In his *Concise Theology* Packer puts it, well, concisely: 'God's justifying decision is the judgment of the Last Day, declaring where we shall spend eternity, brought forward into the present and pronounced here and now.'[7]

Heaven Is In Us

So we see just how true it is to say that the Christian is an already heavenly man: his disposition, his desires and his justification all belong to the world above, and yet he possesses them here, already. We sometimes speak of the believer as being 'in the world but not of it'. That is, he lives in this present evil age, but in terms of spiritual life and outlook he does not truly belong to

---

[7] J. I. Packer, *Concise Theology* (Wheaton, Illinois: Tyndale, 1993), p. 165.

it. When it comes to heaven the opposite is true: the believer is 'of heaven but not in it'! It's as if the Christian lives and breathes on earth bathed in an unseen heavenly light, which shines down from above and emanates from within, even before he has arrived there. You see, the Christian is truly a man 'ahead of his time', for his life is already marked by realities that belong most fully to the world to come. Just think, how many high school graduating classes over the years have been told by principals and guest speakers at their commencement ceremonies, 'You are the future.' It is standard graduation speech fare, and in a sense it is true. But how much more fully do those words apply to Christian believers! We are the future. We are the sons and daughters of the age to come (*Luke* 20:34-35). In our lives, the future is already underway. It was said of the Puritan Richard Sibbes,

> Of this blest man, let this just praise be given:
> Heaven was in him, before he was in heaven.

In principle the same is true of every Christian.

We should also note that the heavenly light with which the Christian is enveloped grows brighter over time, for our God and Father causes his children to grow spiritually as they seek him. Paul wrote, 'we all, with unveiled face, beholding the glory of the Lord, are being transformed into the same image from one degree of glory to another' (*2 Cor.* 3:18). The traditional term for this gradual lifelong change is 'sanctification': this is 'the work of God's free grace, whereby we are renewed in the whole man after the image of God, and are enabled more and more to die unto sin, and live unto righteousness' (*Westminster Shorter Catechism* Q. 35). The Christian sets out on his lifelong pilgrimage, newly granted love, joy, peace and other spiritual fruit (*Gal.* 5:22-23), and then with God's help he grows in those same graces. Some Christians grow greatly. No doubt Sibbes was one of them, which is why he was praised in

33

those memorable terms. The one who has lived long in Christ, and grown much in Christian virtues, has much of heaven in him.

2. OUR DYING

The next step the Christian takes in his heavenward journey, he takes in his dying. His body he leaves behind on earth, but his soul goes to heaven. Of course this is a mysterious transition for us to consider, since none of us has made it (that is, none of us here on earth, including you the reader and me the writer). But that makes it no less real, no less certain.

This departure represents the culmination of earthly Christian life. Picture it this way: when a man first comes to Christ he has one foot in heaven, one foot left on earth. But then, for the rest of his life, he slowly shifts his spiritual weight. With the passing of time he grows in love for God, even as he grows nearer to the day when he will enter the presence of God. Finally, in death, he lifts his back foot from earth entirely and steps fully into the world above. At last he is both *of* heaven . . . and *in* it too.

This truth transforms the prospect of death for all who are in Christ. Jesus died for us and now lives for us, therefore we know that death will be the occasion of our going to be with him, free from sin, free from sadness. Because Paul believed this, he could say, 'My desire is to depart and be with Christ, for that is far better' (*Phil.* 1:23). Speaking for all Christians, he could also say, 'we would rather be away from the body and at home with the Lord' (*2 Cor.* 5:8). Because Stephen believed this, he could say just before he died, 'Lord Jesus, receive my spirit' (*Acts* 7:59). Because we also believe this, we can sing:

> Death cannot destroy for ever;
> From our fears, cares, and tears
>   It will us deliver.

It will close life's mournful story,
Make a way that we may
Enter heav'nly glory.[8]

Thus the Christian need not cower in the face of death the way many do. He knows that death, though still an end, now represents an even better beginning. In an earlier work I put it this way:

It is not that death is now pleasant. Let us not pretend that it is. But the wonder of the gospel is that grace has conquered and enlisted even the dreadful things of the curse to advance the Saviour's cause. Death is still rightly called 'the last enemy' (*1 Cor.* 15:26), but for the believer the last enemy has already been transformed thanks to the grace of our greatest Friend.[9]

The experience of those in heaven now is what theologians have traditionally referred to as 'the intermediate state'. It is intermediate because (1) *chronologically* it represents an intervening period between life on earth and life in the new creation after the return of Christ, and (2) *qualitatively* it amounts to an improvement (a vast improvement!) on earthly life but is still incomplete compared to the world to come after Christ's return. The believer who has gone to heaven through death has moved up . . . but not all the way up: he remains without a body ('unclothed' as Paul puts it in *2 Cor.* 5:4), plus heaven remains removed from earth, plus God's holy ones in heaven must await the complete ingathering of all his elect and the final putting down of humanity's rebellion against God.

What is life like in heaven now, in this intermediate state? We must admit our knowledge of that world is somewhat shadowy,

---

[8] 'Why Should Cross and Trial Grieve Me?' English translation of words by Paul Gerhardt.

[9] Paul D. Wolfe, *My God Is True! Lessons Learned Along Cancer's Dark Road* (Edinburgh: Banner of Truth, 2009, repr.), p. 127.

but we do know this much: heaven at present is a place of purity, praise, peace and pining. Revelation, that book of fantastic images at the close of the New Testament canon, gives us glimpses of those four realities:

1. Purity: Near the close of Revelation the Apostle John recounts a vision he was given of the heavenly Jerusalem, 'the holy city' (*Rev.* 21:10). He describes the unblemished purity of the place: 'nothing unclean will ever enter it, nor anyone who does what is detestable or false, but only those who are written in the Lamb's book of life' (21:27). This must also be true of heaven at present—'nothing unclean'.

What does this mean for the believer? Well, if he is to gain admission to that most holy world then his own transformation into a state of holiness must first be made complete. After all, there can be 'nothing unclean' about his own heart and ways if he is to be let in. Thankfully, this is precisely what takes place in the Christian when he dies: marvellously, death serves as the occasion of the completion of his sanctification by a mighty, completing act of divine power. When the Christian came to faith in Christ during earthly life he was fully freed from the *guilt* of sin, but only upon his death is he completely liberated from the very *presence* of sin. All vestiges of rebellion against God and reluctance to serve him are finally eradicated from the believer's heart, leaving nothing but holy devotion and desires. Thus believers in heaven are now described as 'the spirits of the righteous made perfect' (*Heb.* 12:23). We noted before that when the believer dies, at last he is both *of* heaven and *in* it too. Here we add this: when he dies he becomes more *of* heaven than he has ever been, for in death he leaves sin behind altogether. Thus is he made ready to step into the presence of God. And when he does, he finds that he has stepped into a world where no traces of sin are to be found. He looks around (at heaven's other inhabitants, both human and angelic), and he looks within (at his own heart)—he even looks upon Christ himself—and what meets his gaze is nothing but unstained holiness in every direction.

2. Praise: 'And the four living creatures . . . never cease to say, "Holy, holy, holy, is the Lord God Almighty, who was and is and is to come!"' (*Rev.* 4:8), and those described as 'the twenty-four elders' join in: 'Worthy are you, our Lord and God, to receive glory and honour and power, for you created all things, and by your will they existed and were created' (4:11). No, we cannot imagine praise offered by disembodied spirits, for the only praise we have ever experienced has been that of embodied creatures, including ourselves, but heaven must resound with such 'songs' in some wonderful fashion. In short, they *praise* as never before because they *see* as never before. First, they behold the Son of God, Jesus Christ, in his glorified human nature. Second, they enjoy a new spiritual intimacy with the Triune Godhead. That is, God manifests his glory with a fullness that we on earth have never known, and in their perfect holiness they are capable of taking it all in. Sometimes this is referred to as the 'beatific vision'. No, this vision of the Triune God is not physical; it is spiritual. But that hardly makes it less than real. To the contrary, it must be the most real and wonderful 'sight' of all!

3. Peace: 'And I heard a voice from heaven saying, "Write this: Blessed are the dead who die in the Lord from now on." "Blessed indeed", says the Spirit, "that they may rest from their labours, for their deeds follow them!"' (14:13). On earth they laboured as those striving for Christ in spite of sin within and opposition without, but now they strive no more. On earth they waged spiritual warfare, but now they have laid down their arms.

4. Pining: 'They cried out with a loud voice, "O Sovereign Lord, holy and true, how long before you will judge and avenge our blood on those who dwell on the earth?"' (6:10).

'But wait. Do they say that? Really?' Here we can anticipate the same sort of question we considered before in connection to creation: 'Does this mean that heaven isn't perfect? How can anyone who's already gone there be anything less than completely satisfied? There's no sin there, no sorrow, no death. How can they be left longing for more?'

Same question, same answer: it depends upon what you mean by 'perfect'. Do you mean 'as good as it gets'? Then no, heaven isn't perfect, not now. It is perfect in the sense that there is no sin and misery there, and in the sense that it fully suits God's purposes. But his purpose for the present is to delay the righting of all wrongs until the day he has appointed, which means that all his children—even those who have already reached heaven—must wait until some of their desires are satisfied. Even Christ himself can be described as waiting for that day: 'But when Christ had offered for all time a single sacrifice for sins, he sat down at the right hand of God, waiting from that time until his enemies should be made a footstool for his feet' (*Heb.* 10:12-13). Of course, Christ waits with confidence and patience and zeal, and so do his holy ones in heaven wait with him. There is no sadness or disappointment about their yearning, but it is yearning still. When it comes to the ushering in of the new creation and all it entails, they long for it (as we do), but God has said, 'Not yet.'

3. CHRIST'S RETURNING

OK, not yet. So . . . when? When will all wrongs be righted? When will all God's elect ones have been brought in, and clothed with their resurrection bodies, and granted a glorious new world in which to worship and work and play? The short answer is: on the day when Jesus Christ returns from heaven to earth. 'Men of Galilee, why do you stand looking into heaven? This Jesus, who was taken up from you into heaven, will come in the same way as you saw him go into heaven' (*Acts* 1:11). 'Christ, having been offered once to bear the sins of many, will appear a second time, not to deal with sin but to save those who are eagerly waiting for him' (*Heb.* 9:28). On that day . . .

1. Christ will give believers imperishable, glorious, powerful bodies (*1 Cor.* 15:42-43) like the one he received in his own resurrection. He 'will transform our lowly body to be like his glorious body' (*Phil.* 3:21). When it comes to the resurrection body, the Bible leaves much to the imagination, but we can confidently imagine this much: it will be far better than the body we possess in the present. The adjectives imperishable, glorious and powerful in 1 Corinthians 15 certainly indicate improvement! But it will also be marked by continuity with the body we have now: notice that Jesus will '*transform* our lowly body'. In other words, my resurrection body will still be *my* body, but it will be my body *raised*. God will not replace my mortal body, but will give it resurrection life making it mortal no more (*Rom.* 8:11). This was the case with Jesus himself: he was raised in the same body in which he had died, and yet his physicality was clearly of a different order (*John* 20:19). On the day of his return, Jesus will grant all believers to join him in this glorified physicality. How will he do this? The Bible does not say. And yet we can confidently affirm that all believers—those still living at the time of his return and those who had passed into heaven through death—will find themselves newly and wondrously clothed (*1 Cor.* 15:51-53).

What about unbelievers on that dread day? They too will find themselves reunited with their bodies. In his defence before Governor Felix, Paul said that 'there will be a resurrection of both the just and the unjust' (*Acts* 24:15). Just as believers will be bodily raised in a way that fits them for the glories of the new world, so unbelievers will be bodily raised in a way that fits them for the judgment that awaits them. The final bodies of God's children will be as royal robes. The final bodies of God's enemies will be as prison garb. This truth may be hard for us to hear, but we hear it from the lips of Jesus himself. He said, 'Do not marvel at this, for an hour is coming when all who are in the tombs will hear his voice and come out, those who have done good to the resurrection of life, and those who have done evil to the resurrection of judgment' (*John* 5:28-29).

2. Christ will judge the world. On the one hand, he will 'openly acknowledge and acquit' (language we noted before from the *Westminster Shorter Catechism*) all those who trusted and served him. Our salvation will be attributable to divine grace from first to last, including this: on that day Christ will point to the obedience we rendered in this life, which was the fruit of grace, as the evidence of our genuine faith in him (*Matt.* 25:31-45; *Eph.* 2:8-10). See the genius of the gospel: God will show himself to be one who loves our good works . . . at the same time that he saves us on the basis of Christ's works and not our own! Masterful. On the other hand, in that same judgment Christ will put all wrongs to right by exacting judgment on those who remained in rebellion against their Maker, including those who manifested that rebellion by their mistreatment of Christians (*2 Thess.* 1:6-10).

Related to the judgment of the last day, we should also note that in the new world each Christian will come into the treasures he stored up during his lifetime of service before death. 'Do not lay up for yourselves treasures on earth, where moth and rust destroy and where thieves break in and steal, but lay up for yourselves treasures in heaven' (*Matt.* 6:19-20). Similarly, Paul refers to the 'reward' that awaits believers who build well on Christ's foundation, as opposed to the 'loss' (that is, the relative lack of reward) in store for believers who build poorly (*1 Cor.* 3:14-15). Though Christians dare not cower before the prospect of final judgment, fearing that eternal condemnation awaits them (for it does not: 'There is therefore now no condemnation for those who are in Christ Jesus'—*Rom.* 8:1), still we must take seriously the truth that our loving and holy Father cares about our obedience (or lack of it) in this life, and has promised to honour each of his children according to that obedience. 'For we will all stand before the judgment seat of God', says Paul, and 'each of us will give an account of himself to God' (*Rom.* 14:10, 12). Understood aright, it ought to be stirring and not terrifying to learn that beyond this life Christians''deeds will follow them'(*Rev.* 14:13). Indeed, this is pronounced in that same Revelation verse as an aspect of their blessedness: 'And I heard a voice from heaven saying, "Write this: Blessed are the dead who die in the Lord from now on.""Blessed indeed", says the Spirit, "that they may rest from their labours, for their deeds follow them!"' Of course, even the rewards our Father bestows will be gifts of his grace, for even the best obedience on our part does not merit reward (*Luke* 17:10). What a generous Father we serve! This puts to rest the suspicion that there is something selfish about desiring and receiving God-given honours for our good works: not only has Christ called us to this (and therefore it cannot be selfish), but also our rewards will redound to God's praise in the end.

Precisely what these rewards will be and how they will shape life in the new creation, Scripture does not say. The Spirit has been content to tantalize us! The question is, will we trust him that great things must be in store? This much we can say: the new world will be one of remarkable and fascinating variety, even among the redeemed, each honoured in his own way, some more, some less. And yet none will sense lack, for each will be full of glory to his own capacity, plus each will lovingly rejoice in (instead of envying) the different capacities and honours of others. Jonathan Edwards put it this way:

> Not the least remainder of any principle of envy shall exist to
> be exercised toward angels or other beings who are superior
> in glory; nor shall there be aught like contempt or slighting of

those who are inferiors. Those that have a lower station in glory than others, suffer no diminution of their own happiness by seeing others above them in glory. On the contrary, all the members of that blessed society rejoice in each other's happiness, for the love of benevolence is perfect in them all. Every one has not only a sincere, but a perfect good-will to every other.[10]

Can we even imagine such a rich and rewarding society? Imagine it . . . for it is coming!

3. Christ will renew the world—I mean, *this* world—so as to make it a fitting dwelling place for God's renewed people. Admittedly, 2 Peter 3 uses cataclysmic language to describe what will happen to the created order on the last day ('burning, dissolution, melting'). But that language is fairly understood to describe a dramatic renewal of the current creation, not its elimination, since the Scriptures elsewhere speak of the world to come in terms that suggest continuity with the world as we know it now. For example, the Lord promised his royal Son, 'Ask of me, and I will make the nations your heritage, and the ends of the earth your possession' (*Psa.* 2:8), and the Son later made the same promise to his disciples: 'Blessed are the meek, for they shall inherit the earth' (*Matt.* 5:5). In the end we will come into our inheritance. Just as my resurrection body will be my body raised, so will the new world be this world glorified. Lo and behold, the promised 'new earth' (*Isa.* 65:17) will turn out to be this earth made new. The redeemed have been made 'a kingdom and priests to our God, and they shall reign on the earth' (*Rev.* 5:10). What do we say when a friend gives us a tour of his impressively remodelled home? 'I love what you've done with the place.' How much more will we say that—or at least think that, for the beauty of the sight may leave us speechless—when we first behold on that great day what

---

[10] Jonathan Edwards, 'Heaven, A World of Charity or Love', in *Charity and Its Fruits* (Edinburgh: Banner of Truth, 1998), p. 335.

this world was always meant to be. 'My Saviour, my Friend, how I love what you've done with this place. And to think that you've done it for me!'

These, then, are the works that Christ will perform upon his return: bodily resurrection, kingly judgment and cosmic renewal. The end result will be the 'new heavens and a new earth in which righteousness dwells' (*2 Pet.* 3:13) that God's people have always longed for. This is what theologians have traditionally referred to as 'the eternal state' (in distinction from the intermediate state we considered before). We will know God with unprecedented fullness and intimacy. We will love God with eternal love, never to fall away. We will see Christ even as we resemble him. We will have bodies that fully serve our intentions. We will live and serve fruitfully on solid ground. Life without fear, labour without frustration. Picking up on Paul's personification in Romans 8, the ground itself will no longer groan but rejoice, and we will rejoice with it. 'The old has passed away; behold, the new has come' (*2 Cor.* 5:17). 'He will wipe away every tear from their eyes, and death shall be no more, neither shall there be mourning, nor crying, nor pain anymore, for the former things have passed away' (*Rev.* 21:4).

GOOD/BETTER/BEST

Look back now upon the three stages we have covered in this chapter.

1. Knowing Christ in this life is *good* (very good).

2. Going to be with Christ after death is *better* ('far better', as Paul puts it in *Phil.* 1:23).

3. Life on the new earth will be *best* of all.

The *Westminster Larger Catechism* puts it this way:

1. Knowing Christ in this life amounts to enjoying the *firstfruits* of our heavenly communion with him (*WLC* Q. 83).

2. Going to be with Christ after death means *further* communion with him (*WLC* Q. 85).

3. Life on the new earth will feature *full* communion with our Saviour at last (*WLC* Q. 90).

'Firstfruits', then 'further', then 'full'. On the day when Jesus returns, he will usher in that full communion!

'Yes', you say, 'but when will *that* be? Precisely when will Jesus come back and do all this?' 'But concerning that day and hour no one knows, not even the angels of heaven, nor the Son, but the Father only' (*Matt.* 24:36). So taught Jesus during his earthly ministry, and certainly nothing has taken place since then to reveal the answer to us! The Christian is called to live with eagerness for the new creation, even though he does not know precisely when and how it will be inaugurated. That eagerness is part of what it means to be heavenly-minded. And that brings us to Chapter 3 . . .

CHAPTER THREE

Set Your Minds

CHRISTIAN musical artist Charlie Peacock wrote and sang a song featuring this memorable line: 'I want to live like heaven is a real place.' The Apostles Paul and Peter wanted to live that way too. In fact, they wanted that not only for themselves but also for the Christians they cared for in congregations scattered around the Mediterranean world. Paul and Peter knew that heaven is a real place, and they wanted the sons and daughters of heaven to live in the light of that truth. Plus, they knew that right living begins with right thinking. Here are three passages in their writings in which they called Christians to heavenly-mindedness.

1. 2 Corinthians 4:17–18

> For this light momentary affliction is preparing for us an eternal weight of glory beyond all comparison, as we look not to the things that are seen but to the things that are unseen. For the things that are seen are transient, but the things that are unseen are eternal.

In these words we have one of the New Testament's most resounding manifestos of heavenly-mindedness. Here Paul is describing the outlook that he and his fellow gospel workers have made their own, but this is no uniquely apostolic mindset. Paul has in view something that is, and ought to be, true of all Christians.

Did you notice Paul's peculiar expression in the middle of that passage? 'We look . . . to the things that are unseen.' So says the Apostle Paul: we see the unseen! If his words make any sense, he must have a spiritual kind of seeing in view. Paul prayed for the Ephesians along these lines: 'having the eyes of your hearts enlightened, that you may know what is the hope to which he has called you, what are the riches of his glorious inheritance in the saints, and what is the immeasurable greatness of his power toward us who believe' (*Eph.* 1:18-19). Notice, with 'the eyes of their hearts' Christians behold invisible realities.

Back to 2 Corinthians 4, just what are the 'things unseen' to which Paul is referring? His broad, unqualified language invites us to fill in the meaning fully. Our heavenly Father is unseen, the one 'whom no one has ever seen or can see' (*1 Tim.* 6:16), and the same is true of the Son and the Spirit (the incarnate Son with respect to his divinity). Jesus Christ is presently unseen, not because he is spirit only (remember, he is now clothed with a human nature, body included), but because he has gone to a place removed from our own. The angels and saints in heaven are unseen, because they are there and not here, plus they are not embodied as we are. The world to come is unseen, because it remains an unrealized future prospect. Paul is saying, we look to these things.

Notice, as well, that 'looking to them' means more than possessing a mere awareness that these things are real. After all, Paul's purpose in this passage is not simply to remind the Corinthians of invisible realities, but to show them how those realities give comfort to those who are 'afflicted . . . perplexed . . . persecuted . . . struck down' (verses 8-9), those whose 'outer self is wasting away' (verse 16), those who face the temptation to 'lose heart' (verses 1, 16). Looking to things unseen means prizing them—prizing them above all others—and doing so knowing that we have gained them. We look to unseen realities knowing that we ourselves belong to that unseen world, that that world is destined to be seen one day, revealed in glory, like never before, and that we shall be revealed with it (*Rom.* 8:19).

2. *Colossians 3:1-4*

If then you have been raised with Christ, seek the things that are above, where Christ is, seated at the right hand of God. Set your minds on things that are above, not on things that are on earth. For you have died, and your life is hidden with Christ in God. When Christ who is your life appears, then you also will appear with him in glory.

We just looked at 2 Corinthians 4, in which Paul referred to 'things that are unseen'. Here he points the Colossians to 'things that are above'. The wording is different, but the meaning is basically the same. And the calling is the same too: 'set your minds' means more than acknowledging that these things are real; it means focusing on them, prizing them, seeking them. Paul even puts it that way in the beginning: 'seek the things that are above'. Observe as well, at the end of the passage, that Paul points the Colossians forward to their heavenly future. One day Christ will appear, he says, and when he does we will appear with him: we will not just be with him; we will shine like him, reflecting his glory as sons and daughters of the resurrection who finally resemble our Elder Brother.

In stark contrast to these words in Colossians stands Paul's warning to the Philippians concerning those who 'walk as enemies of the cross of Christ' (*Phil.* 3:18). How does Paul characterize these enemies? 'Their end is destruction, their god is their belly, and they glory in their shame', and then he adds these words: *'with minds set on earthly things'* (verse 19). When Paul accuses them of setting their minds on earthly things, clearly he is not referring to a God-honouring attention to earthly matters, the sort of mind-setting that is necessary in our daily callings. (Lawyer, focus on law. Chef, focus on food. Driver, focus on the road.) No, he is exposing an idolatrous, God-denying obsession with those matters. Do you see how serious the stakes are? Setting our minds on heavenly things or earthly things as our chief concern in life is a matter of serving Christ or opposing him—a matter of spiritual 'friend or foe'—and there is no neutral ground.

3. 1 Peter 1:13

> Therefore, preparing your minds for action, and being sober-minded, set your hope fully on the grace that will be brought to you at the revelation of Jesus Christ.

Here Peter focuses on the future, and he urges his readers to 'set their hope fully' on that future day. Of course, the Christian will look forward to earthly days down the road and to what those days may bring. This is perfectly natural. But his ultimate horizon will always rest beyond this life, even beyond death at the end of this life, to the day of Christ's return. He anticipates that day with fullness, knowing that his anticipation will be fully vindicated.

SET YOUR MINDS

Piece these and other Scripture texts together, and we come to these conclusions. What does heavenly-mindedness entail? It entails: meditation, orientation and anticipation. What fruits does it bear? It bears the fruits of consecration and supplication. Let us consider each of these in turn.

1. Meditation

This is the heart of the matter. First and foremost, being heavenly-minded means thinking about heaven. After all, it can hardly be said that you are 'mindful' of something if your *mind* is never *full* of that something!

Psalm 1 says this about the truly blessed man: 'his delight is in the law of the LORD, and on his law he meditates day and night' (verse 2). In other words, he makes God's Word the object of his continuing contemplations. He takes time to think about what God is like and about what he has done: 'On the glorious splendour of your majesty, and on your wondrous works, I will meditate' (*Psa.* 145:5). To meditate upon God's Word, God's glory and God's works certainly includes contemplating what his Word teaches about heaven.

For some the word 'meditation' brings to mind something resembling the practices of Eastern religions: light a candle, sit quietly, breathe deeply, close your eyes, and clear your mind, perhaps to the sounds of soothing music. That is not my meaning here. By 'meditation' I simply mean taking the time to give some subject your purposeful attention. Biblical meditation is not a matter of stilling the body and emptying the mind, but filling the mind with God's truth in order carefully to consider that truth and bring it home to the heart. And that can be done sitting or standing, when jogging or driving, while washing dishes or folding laundry, body in motion and eyes wide open. The one who meditates upon the gospel holds it before his eyes like a multi-faceted jewel, turning it slowly so as to gaze upon its many sides as they catch the light. The Christian ought to treat the truth of heaven this way: deliberately holding it before his mind and slowly turning it round so as to see its many aspects. In Chapters 1 and 2 we did just that: we considered the glories of heaven from various angles: chronological and theological, divine and human, present and future. We slowly turned and studied the jewel.

Are these realities not worthy of our contemplation? Of course they are. Listen to John Calvin:

we who claim to have a personal religion must call to mind that this present life will not last and will soon be over. We should spend it thinking about immortality. Now, eternal and immortal life can be found nowhere except in God. It follows, then that the main care and concern of our life should be to seek God. We should long for him with all the affection of our hearts, and not find rest and peace anywhere except in him alone.[1]

What a striking way of putting it: we should spend this present life thinking about immortality. In his *Institutes of the Christian Religion* Calvin says this even more strongly: looking forward to the resurrection of believers at the end of the age, he comments, 'he alone has fully profited in the gospel who has accustomed himself to continual meditation upon the blessed resurrection'.[2] Obviously Calvin does not mean that we should spend every waking moment thinking about heaven, just as the phrase 'day and night' in Psalm 1 does not imply that. Instead, the meaning is that we ought to think regularly about heaven, and then allow those thoughts to inform how we spend all our other moments. No, we will not be those who sit around all day and do nothing but think about heaven, pausing only to eat, sleep and bathe. How empty and unsatisfying such a life would be—even if the food is very good! Rather, we will be those who take time to think and pray, and who then rise up renewed to live full-orbed human lives.

Of course, to commit ourselves to this kind of deliberate thoughtfulness is to swim against the cultural tide. In our noisy, fast-paced, gut-instinct, short-attention-span society, the very idea of stopping to think about anything has fallen on hard times, especially thinking about anything unseen. The broader culture can push us

[1] John Calvin, *Truth for All Time: A Brief Outline of the Christian Faith*, tr. Stuart Olyott (Edinburgh: Banner of Truth, 2008), p. 2.
[2] John Calvin, *Institutes of the Christian Religion*, ed. John T. McNeill, tr. Ford Lewis Battles, vol. 2 (Philadelphia: Westminster Press, 1960), p. 988.

away from maintaining a proper meditative mindset. And closer to home, the culture of the Christian church may do the same. Because the Bible is the Word of God—a Word we so desperately need to teach, reprove, correct and train us—some Christians seem to assume that, when it comes to Bible intake, there is no such thing as too much. Sunday morning sermon, plus Sunday school lesson, plus another Sunday sermon if the church meets in the evening, plus at least one weekly Bible study, plus daily private Bible reading, plus family devotions, plus theological reading in the evening. But does the Christian ever take time to stop and think about anything he has read or heard? Perhaps he will take time while in the car, driving to work or running errands, to reflect upon lessons recently learned. No, of course he won't: when you're in the car you're supposed to be listening to more sermons on CD! The end result, unfortunately, is what might be termed 'spiritual indigestion'.[3] So much spiritual food, but none of it properly processed. So much consumed, yet so little resultant health and strength.

Christian, follow the prescription of our Great Physician: at some point you have got to stop reading, stop listening, and start *thinking*. Put down your book, press pause on your audio player, and think about what you have taken in. Reflect. Ponder. Dwell. Linger. I understand sometimes a book is so fascinating or so encouraging that you read it in one sitting, but do you devour all your books that way, and then promptly move on to the next one?

A favourite story in our family is that of *The Incredible Book Eating Boy*, a children's story written and illustrated by Oliver Jeffers.[4] *The Incredible Book Eating Boy* tells the tale of a little boy named Henry who develops the habit of—you guessed it—eating books. 'He wasn't sure at first, and tried eating a single word, just

---

[3] Thanks to fellow minister David Coffin for this helpful—and slightly unsettling—way of describing it.

[4] Oliver Jeffers, *The Incredible Book Eating Boy* (New York: Philomel Books, 2006).

to test. Next, he tried a whole sentence and then the whole page. Yes, Henry definitely liked them. By Wednesday, he had eaten a WHOLE book. And by the end of the month he could eat a whole book in one go.' Like most addicts, over time Henry needs more to satisfy his cravings: 'He went from eating books whole to eating them three or four at a time. Books about anything. Henry wasn't fussy, and he wanted to know it all.' Not surprisingly, the happy days of Henry's devouring soon turn sour. 'But then things started going not quite so well. In fact, they started going very, very wrong. Henry was eating too many books, and too quickly at that.' Instead of invigorated he begins to feel ill. Instead of smart he begins to get things all mixed up. The story does have a happy ending—Henry learns to read books and eat broccoli instead (a doubly happy ending, all mothers would agree)—but he certainly learned his lesson the hard way.[5]

Unfortunately, Henry's voracious consumption of books, never pausing to digest, captures all too well the way some Christians relate to God's truth, whether read or heard. And that includes God's truth about heaven. Of course, for obvious reasons, I would not want to discourage you from reading books about heaven. But I do want to discourage you, most earnestly, from reading without ever thinking. If that means placing a bookmark in this book right now and going for a walk, do it. I'll be here when you get back. Have you ever taken two uninterrupted minutes—just two minutes—to think about how wonderful heaven is going to be? If not, why not go for that walk right now and give it a try? And then make it a habit. If only for a brief moment each day, practice the art of pondering: hold some aspect of the gospel before the eyes of your heart, take a good, long look . . . and rejoice!

[5] Go out and buy this book even if you do not have small children in the house. The illustrations are priceless. My providing snippets of the text hardly does it justice. The book is even published with a small bite cut out of the corner of the back cover!

In his discussion of Christian meditation in his work *The Christian's Daily Walk,* the Puritan Henry Scudder makes this claim: 'For according to a person's meditation such is he.'[6] In other words, a person's meditation defines his character. Is that claim too strong? No. What a man thinks about—that is, what he thinks about often, and carefully, and longingly—surely reflects the kind of man he is. So, would you be heavenly? Think about it.

2. Orientation

Remember the words from Psalm 1 we noted before concerning the truly blessed man: 'his delight is in the law of the LORD, and on his law he meditates day and night' (verse 2). We have already concentrated on the 'meditates' part. Now let us consider the 'delight' part. He *delights* in the law of the Lord. In other words, he meditates upon it as one who is drawn to it. Suggest to him that he think about God's Word, and he does not turn up his nose. Instead he jumps at the opportunity. Indeed, you may very well find he was already thinking about it before you urged him. In principle this is the case when it comes to the Christian and reflecting on heaven. In short, he looks to heaven as one who loves heaven. Remember, he has those new heavenly desires we considered in Chapter 2. I say this is true of the Christian 'in principle' because, as every Christian knows, sometimes his heavenly desires wane, and sometimes other factors distract and discourage him. But even then, deep down, this new orientation abides.

Old Testament believers, though miles removed from Jerusalem, were still Jerusalem-minded. More precisely, they were temple-minded. When he dedicated the newly built temple in Jerusalem, Solomon anticipated the day when distant Israelites would pray

---

[6] Henry Scudder, *The Christian's Daily Walk in Holy Security and Peace* (Harrisonburg, Virginia: Sprinkle Publications, 1984), p. 102. Cf. Proverbs 23:7: 'For as he thinketh in his heart, so is he' (AV).

'toward' the temple (*1 Kings* 8:48). This serves as a picture of the Christian's relationship to heaven: at present he is removed from it, but he always has a sense of facing it, especially when he prays. For the Old Testament believer, facing the temple meant (symbolically speaking) facing God, because the temple stood for the presence of God among his people. How much truer is that of the Christian! Heaven is the place where God is best known, thus the Christian lives and prays pointed toward that place. 'But you have come to Mount Zion and to the city of the living God, the heavenly Jerusalem' (*Heb.* 12:22). 'But the Jerusalem above is free, and she is our mother' (*Gal.* 4:26).

Imagine someone who now lives in a country other than his native land, someone for whom his homeland remains a beloved place. Perhaps you know someone in that circumstance. Perhaps you *are* that someone! He feels as if there is a compass within him that points, not north, but home. He regularly thinks of his native land—and even when he is occupied with other concerns the place of his birth is not far away, just in the back of his mind—because he is, in a sense, still facing that land. He is oriented toward it. So it is with the Christian: his heart now points heavenward, and thus his mind is now drawn upward. In fact, for the Christian this orientation is something far better: his is not the pining of a man removed from a place in his past, uncertain if he will ever return; the Christian faces his *future* home, and he can be absolutely certain of arriving there. The earthly expatriate remembers where he was and may never be again. The Christian looks to a place he has never been, but where he will live forever.

3. Anticipation

Here is one more aspect of what it means to be heavenly-minded: not only does the Christian think about heaven, and not only does he think about it as one drawn to it, but he also thinks about heaven as one *destined* for it. Heavenly-mindedness equals meditation plus orientation . . . plus anticipation. He sets his mind on the world above eager to be there, and confident that one day he will be. And because the day of his death and the day of Christ's return are both unknown to him (*Luke* 12:20; *Matt.* 25:13), his anticipation is both ready and watchful.

Remember how both Paul and Peter stoked the fires of anticipation in the three Bible passages we studied at the beginning of this chapter: Paul spoke of 'an eternal weight of glory beyond all comparison' being prepared for us (*2 Cor.* 4:17); Paul spoke of believers appearing with Christ 'in glory' on the day of his appearing (*Col.* 3:4); and Peter directed his readers to 'the grace that will be brought to you at the revelation of Jesus Christ' (*1 Pet.* 1:13).

To those three anticipation passages add three more. Paul reminds the Thessalonians 'how you turned to God from idols to serve the living and true God, and to wait for his Son from heaven, whom he raised from the dead, Jesus who delivers us from the wrath to come' (*1 Thess.* 1:9-10). Paul tells the Philippians, 'But our citizenship is in heaven, and from it we await a Saviour, the Lord Jesus Christ' (*Phil.* 3:20). Paul tells Titus that, thanks to the grace of God, we are those 'waiting for our blessed hope, the appearing of the glory of our great God and Saviour Jesus Christ' (*Titus* 2:13). You see, the longing expressed by the Psalmist—'my soul waits for the Lord more than watchmen for the morning' (*Psa.* 130:6)—now has Christ himself as its object.

What is striking about these New Testament passages is that the apostles so often pointed Christians all the way forward to the return of Jesus. You see, there is more to the Christian's hope than, 'I'm going to go be with Jesus when I die.' When it comes to heaven what matters most is not our going (at death) but his coming (at the end of the age). Still, our going does matter. We anticipate that momentous step too—the step we will take in dying.

The Christian does feel a proper sense of longing for the blessedness of heaven now, and it is that longing that enables him—or ought to enable him—to face death without falling apart at the seams. The end of my life, and the end of the age. Neither of those is a small step. Both are giant leaps!

The question might be posed: 'If heaven is going to be so wonderful, and if death is the occasion of our going there, then why shouldn't the Christian simply end his own life and get there right away?' In other words, why wait? No doubt some deeply confused Christians have posed that question to themselves only to find they had no satisfactory answer, with tragic results. Here are two answers. First, the Lord has given us his sixth commandment—'You shall not murder' (*Exod.* 20:13)—of which suicide is a violation. Second, the Lord has also given us wholesome desires to remain in this life, serving others. If those desires have waned within us, then we ought to nurture them back to health. This is why the Christian feels conflicting emotions about life and death, earth and heaven. The Apostle Paul admitted to feeling such mixed emotions himself: 'If I am to live in the flesh, that means fruitful labour for me. Yet which I shall choose I cannot tell. I am hard pressed between the two. My desire is to depart and be with Christ, for that is far better. But to remain in the flesh is more necessary on your account' (*Phil.* 1:22-24). Paul sets us a valuable example here. It is not that the Christian's sense of heavenly anticipation ought to be dulled or diminished, but that it is rightly accompanied by other strong desires. Take heart: feeling torn like Paul is actually a sign of spiritual health!

4. Consecration

Meditation. Orientation. Anticipation. These make up biblical heavenly-mindedness. And that mindset bears fruit. It shows. It shows in this, first of all: consecration. 'Consecration' belongs to that family of Bible words all containing the root idea of being set apart unto God, words like 'hallowed', 'holy', 'sacred', and 'sancti-fied'. To the degree that a man is fixed on heaven, conscious that he already belongs to heaven, he will give himself now to holy, heavenly living.

One more time, consider Peter's words in 1 Peter 1:13: 'Therefore, preparing your minds for action, and being sober-minded, set your hope fully on the grace that will be brought to you at the revela-tion of Jesus Christ.' At first glance this might seem like a rather peculiar statement. Peter seems to be saying something like, 'Get ready . . . get set . . . *wait!*' We might have expected something a bit more active, a bit more here-and-now: 'Get ready . . . get set . . . get busy being holy right away.' Well, Peter does proceed to talk about holiness. He does so in the very next verses: 'As obedient children, do not be conformed to the passions of your former igno-rance, but as he who called you is holy, you also be holy in all your conduct' (verses 14-15). But before he tells them 'be holy', first he tells them 'be hopeful'. In other words, before he turns his atten-tion and theirs to present moral concerns, he directs their gaze to future heavenly expectations. Why do this? Peter does not explain his train of thought, but we know this much: there is an intimate relationship between hopefulness for the future and holiness in the present. Hopefulness encourages holiness. How so? To set your hope fully on the grace to be brought to you at the revelation of Jesus Christ is to be reminded that giving yourself to the cause of holiness in the present is not to pledge yourself to a lost cause, to a doomed campaign. That cause will most certainly prevail, for the day of Christ's revelation, when holiness will triumph, is certainly scheduled on the divine calendar. Putting sin to death and rising in righteousness instead takes hard work, but that work will not be in vain.

The concerns of consecration come out in Peter's Second Letter too. In 2 Peter 3 he describes in fantastic terms the renewal of the world that will take place at the end of the age, and then he says, 'Since all these things are thus to be dissolved, what sort of people ought you to be in lives of holiness and godliness' (*2 Pet.* 3:11). A few verses later he says it again: 'Therefore, beloved, since you are waiting for these, be diligent to be found by him without spot or blemish, and at peace' (verse 14). So this is yet another Bible verse to add to our growing list of verses in which Christians are described as 'waiting' for the end of the age, but do you see that healthy Christian waiting is no idle 'waiting around'? Peter says, in effect, 'You are waiting for a world of righteousness (verse 13). Well then, get started on righteousness. Right now. No need to wait for that!'

This helps answer the tired old charge that 'those who are heavenly-minded are of no earthly good'. Remember, biblical consecration is more than a matter of saying 'no' in the face of particular temptations. Biblical holiness is positive as well as negative. God calls us to say 'yes' to the world he has made, which means making the most of its potential and thereby seeking to glorify him in every aspect of human experience. 'For everything created by God is good, and nothing is to be rejected if it is received with thanksgiving' (*1 Tim.* 4:4). 'So, whether you eat or drink, or whatever you do, do all to the glory of God' (*1 Cor.* 10:31). The consecration that real heavenly-mindedness fosters does not amount to checking out on the world—indeed, that is no real consecration!—but to pouring oneself into the service of God in every responsibility, every relationship, every moment. In the beginning God made man to do just that, and the mandate remains. Those who have set their minds on the world to come take up that creation-affirming mandate with new vigour.

5. Supplication

The one who thinks on heaven, who is drawn to it and destined for it, asks for it. This is what 'supplication' means: earnest, humble entreaty. No, the Christian does not ask for death—at least, he shouldn't. True, Elijah and Jonah asked to die (*1 Kings* 19:4; *Jon.* 4:3), but in that respect they were no role models. The Christian does not ask to die, but he does ask for the return of Jesus. These are nearly the very last words in 1 Corinthians: 'Our Lord, come!' (*1 Cor.* 16:22). These are nearly the very last words in the whole Bible: 'He who testifies to these things says, "Surely I am coming soon." Amen. Come, Lord Jesus!' (*Rev.* 22:20). This is the Christian's desire, and he says so. He says so to God. He asks this of God.

As we just saw, this is not the Christian's only desire. Like Paul he also has aspirations to remain and serve, plus he longs to see others come to faith in Christ just as he has. And because the Christian's desires run the gamut, so do his petitions. Remember, 'prayer is an offering up of our desires unto God' (*Westminster Shorter Catechism* Q. 98). Still, this is one of them: 'Come, Lord Jesus.' The Christian may not put it precisely in those terms. He may say something different, something like 'Your kingdom come' (*Matt.* 6:10). But of course you can hardly pray for the coming of the kingdom of God without thereby praying for the coming of God's King. Think about that the next time you pray the Lord's Prayer!

CHECK YOUR PULSE

So, what does heavenly-mindedness entail? It entails: meditation, orientation and anticipation. What fruits does it bear? It bears the fruits of consecration and supplication.

Now that we have made our way through this material, check your pulse. What does your spiritual heart rate monitor reveal about your own level of heavenly-mindedness? Do you ever think about heaven? Do you find yourself drawn to think about it? Do you long to be there? Do you see evidences of consecration? Do you hear the sounds of supplication? I mean, can you even hear yourself saying, 'Come, Lord Jesus'? Have you ever said that to God, or words like it?

Sometimes our pulse does grow faint. For every Christian there are days and seasons like that. Hopefully what you read in the pages that follow will get your heart (and mine) beating again with proper pace and strength. To that end, in the next chapter we will consider some of the ways in which heavenly-mindedness makes a valuable difference in the day-to-day lives of God's people.

CHAPTER FOUR

Down to Earth

THE truths of heaven are meant to touch down in our earthly lives in a host of ways. Every area of life is to be permeated with heavenly light. In this chapter we will consider several of those areas. In keeping with the first commandment of Christian teaching ('Thou shalt alliterate'), you will notice they all begin with 'M': (1) Marriage; (2) Money and Moving; and (3) Miseries and Mistreatment.

1. MARRIAGE

Peter urged husbands to honour their wives 'since they are heirs with you of the grace of life' (*1 Pet.* 3:7). Fellow Christians united in marriage are also fellow pilgrims, making their way to glory and certain to arrive there. This truth has the potential to revolutionize any marriage relationship. Imagine the impact it would make.

First, it would instil a sense of aim, a sense of purpose, in marriage. How many Christian couples, years after getting married (in some cases, not many years at all), reach the point of feeling, 'We're not going anywhere'? Though they launched out on married life in a spirit of excitement and adventure, they now feel stuck in a rut of aimless daily and weekly activities. The incessant cycle of laundry has become the metaphor of their relationship: the same things over and over again, not getting anywhere, not making any progress, only wearing out, colours fading, fabrics fraying. Theirs has become a 'Sisyphus' marriage. In Greek mythology, Sisyphus was the man cursed with this sentence: roll a boulder up a hill, and then watch it roll back down, and then roll it back up again, and repeat for all eternity. For some couples in the church, life feels exactly like that. What can we say about such a Christian marriage? If a Christian husband and wife feel they are not going anywhere, it must be they have lost sight of the fact that they are going somewhere. In fact, they are going to the most unimaginably glorious somewhere, and now united in marriage they are going there together. The gospel prescription begins here: learn to see one another as fellow heirs of the grace of life. Let that truth shape the way you relate to one another and order your life together. No, that will not change things overnight. There may be many factors at work, so this may be only one step in what proves to be a long and arduous recovery. But still it is a good—and vital—first step.

Second, grasping this truth will create a climate in the home in which husband and wife rebuke well, and receive rebukes well. As fellow heirs of the grace of life they are on their way together to perfect holiness, and God's intention is that they should help one another grow in holiness along the way. That includes the willingness to speak with forthrightness and tenderness about sins you have seen in your spouse, and to listen patiently and humbly when your spouse has such words to speak to you. After all, you both have the ultimate goal in view, so you know what those words are for. Heavenly-mindedness tends to lessen harshness and defensiveness in the home and promote gentleness and repentance instead.

Third, grasping this truth will create a climate of hopefulness and optimism. Sadly, in some marriages clouds of cynicism have rolled in. The world is viewed through jaundiced eyes. Husband and wife have become partners in assuming the worst about others . . . including each other. They have become the kind of people that few others want to be around. 'They just seem to be so dour all the time. Frankly, they bring me down.' The hope of heaven, rightly understood and firmly grasped, shines a light that pierces such clouds. The husband and wife who look forward to heaven together realize there is good in the universe—the goodness of God, above all—plus there is something good in store for them which trumps the sin and sadness of this present life. They realize there is cause for brightness and joy after all. They have learned to perceive the positive.

To be clear, this is no Pollyanna outlook, denying the reality of suffering in this life or pretending that suffering does not hurt. Anyone who enters marriage with such an outlook, or tries to recover it later, apparently was not listening to himself on his own wedding day when he vowed faithfulness in circumstances of 'sickness, want and sorrow'. The hope of heaven does not eradicate suffering, but it does put it into perspective. And the Christian couple's perspective is this: wholeness and happiness will have the final word in our lives, and we are on our way there.

Here we should also consider the difference that heaven makes in marriage should God be pleased to give children. During the months before our first children were born (I say 'children' because we started off with twins), my wife and I got away for a brief, just-the-two-of-us, pre-parenthood retreat. Though nothing can quite prepare you for the actual experience of parenthood, we thought it might be a good idea to steal away for a day or two to reflect and pray about what was in store for us. In an effort to bring some focus to our time together, we read and prayed about a sermon preached by Robert Dabney entitled 'Parental Responsibilities'. Dabney's aim in that sermon was to impress upon parents the great weight of their responsibilities toward their children, as well as the unrivalled power they possess to influence their children's lives for good or ill. One consideration that Dabney set before his hearers was this: in God's providence, parents are the instruments for bringing into the world a being that will live forever, either

in eternal blessing or in eternal curse. Read this excerpt, and you
will understand what I mean when I say that our attention was
definitely 'gotten':

> The parent looks upon the tender face which answers to his
> caress with an infantile smile; he should see beneath that smile
> an immortal spark which he has kindled, but can never quench.
> It must grow, for weal or for woe; it cannot be arrested. Just now
> it was not. The parents have mysteriously brought it from dark-
> ness and nothing. There is no power beneath God's throne that
> can remand it back to nothing, should existence prove a curse.
> Yes; the parents have lighted there an everlasting lamp, which
> must burn on when the sun shall have been turned into darkness
> and the moon into blood, either with the glory of heaven or the
> lurid flame of despair.[1]

Those are sobering words, to be sure. But can any Christian
deny they are true? After all, the Bible does not teach that ultimate
blessedness amounts to being absorbed into the Divine so as to
disappear, nor does it teach that ultimate judgment amounts to being annihilated. Either in blessing or in curse, each human being,
once made, will always be. Thus it is the parents' solemn responsibility to strive with every means in hand to lead their children
to eternal blessing, which is knowing the one true God and Jesus
Christ whom he has sent (*John* 17:3).

This consideration, along with others, led Dabney to this conclusion:

> the education of children for God is the most important busi-
> ness done on earth. It is the one business for which the earth
> exists. To it all politics, all war, all literature, all money-making,
> ought to be subordinated; and every parent especially ought to

[1] Robert L. Dabney, 'Parental Responsibilities', in *Discussions*, ed. C. R.
Vaughan, vol. 1 (Harrisonburg, Virginia: Sprinkle Publications, 1994), p. 679.

feel, every hour of the day, that, next to making his own calling and election sure, this is the end for which he is kept alive by God—this is his task on earth.[2]

That order of priorities, would you say it prevails in the world today? No, neither would I. Understandably parents want to provide their children with a rich array of activities and experiences: from soccer practices to piano lessons to museum trips. But how many parents are shuttling their children from one such commitment to the next, stuffing their lives with earthly activities, all the while neglecting—if not completely abandoning—their training for heaven? Of course, parents ought to live rich lives of their own, lives of work and play, developing mind and body, pursuing interests and nurturing relationships. But what if all those engagements have the practical effect of diverting their attention from their children's eternal welfare? The call of the gospel is not to stop working and playing and reading and exercising, nor to remove all the sports and music and field trips from your children's weekly schedule. Rather, the call is this: take time regularly to teach them about God and his gospel. Take time regularly to pray with them and for them. In short, take time to set *their* minds on things above. Borrowing Paul's language in 2 Timothy 3:15, from childhood acquaint them with the sacred writings, which are able to make them wise for salvation through faith in Christ Jesus. Do that, and then all their earthly activities (and yours too) will take on new worth and significance. Whether you eat or drink or play fullback or play violin or study literature or memorize equations, do it all to the glory of God (*1 Cor.* 10:31). Do it all with heaven in view. So may we train our children.

---

[2] Dabney, 'Responsibilities', p. 691.

2. MONEY AND MOVING

Christians ought to handle their earthly wealth (or their relative lack of it) as those whose eyes are fixed on the world to come. Both those who have much and those who have little can become 'graspers', that is, those who cling to money and what money can buy as if this world were the only world that will ever be. Setting our minds on things above sets Christians free from that kind of materialistic desperation. Whether they enjoy plenty or want, they will do so with open hands, holding loosely to what God has provided. Note, that does not mean holding it carelessly, for there are wise and foolish ways of managing our money. For example, the wise man knows about saving patiently (*Prov.* 13:11) and about providing faithfully for the future (*Prov.* 13:22). Rather, it means using God's provisions generously.

This comes out in Paul's instructions to Timothy about how to be a faithful pastor. When Paul teaches Timothy about what to teach the rich, he does not tell Timothy to tell them to stop being rich. Instead, Paul goes for the heart. Those who are wealthy are to demonstrate generosity of spirit: 'charge them not to be haughty, nor to set their hopes on the uncertainty of riches, but on God, who richly provides us with everything to enjoy. They are to do good, to be rich in good works, to be generous and ready to share' (*1 Tim.* 6:17-18). See how the language of 'hope' permeates this passage, both negatively and positively. Negatively: they should not 'set their hopes on the uncertainty of riches'. That is, they dare not look to the future as if their money were the foundation of their future, because that foundation can crumble. For many, it has crumbled. Positively: they should set their hopes 'on God'. That is, they should look to the future trusting in God, trusting that he will certainly bring them into that glorious new world that will be 'full of the knowledge of the LORD as the waters cover the sea' (*Isa.* 11:9).

When it comes to the use of money, the prospect of buying a house and moving looms large. Some say, 'Buying a house is the most important purchase you'll ever make', and there is some truth in that. The moving process comes to my mind because our family recently went through it: preparing our house to sell, and then showing it to potential buyers, and then managing to find a buyer, and then looking at house after house that we might buy and move into, and then settling on one, and finally relocating from the first to the second. Whew! Perhaps I should say we 'endured' that process, or even 'survived' it. As anyone knows who has gone through that ordeal, it brings unique pressures to bear upon the family.

Those pressures are only intensified if you allow yourself to lose sight of your heavenly home. You can find yourself thinking, 'We better get this purchase right, because this may be where we're stuck forever!' ('Excuse me, Christian, did you say "forever"? Aren't you forgetting something? Like death, and heaven, and Jesus, and God?') Put positively, there is something quite liberating about looking forward to heaven while house-hunting on earth. The knowledge that the Lord has in store for me an unimaginably wonderful eternal home keeps me from getting caught up in the real estate rat race in which family budgets are foolishly stretched to the breaking point—if not broken altogether—in a desperate attempt to buy just a few more square feet, just a few additional upgrades, just one more nook for yet another widescreen television. Now, depending upon the circumstances, a larger house with upgrades may be the wise purchase. But of course someday even that larger house will have crumbled, and its upgrades with it, so we dare not fix our hearts there. How different is the Christian's heavenly home, which is 'imperishable, undefiled, and unfading' (*1 Pet.* 1:4). In the real estate business, this is known as 'solid construction'. No wonder, for its 'designer and builder is God' (*Heb.* 11:10).

Far better that your heart be fixed there. 'For where your treasure is, there your heart will be also' (*Matt.* 6:21).

The reality of heaven not only makes a difference when buying a house, it also shapes the way you live in that house in the years that follow. The conviction that heaven is your true home guards you from an idolatrous attachment to the earthly building in which you live now. Instead of seeing it as a fortress to be guarded from invaders (that is, visitors and house guests), or as a museum to be preserved from disturbances (that is, dirt and din), you will see your home as a temporary trust from the Lord to be used in the spirit of hospitality. And hospitality will mean all of the above: occasional visitors and overnight house guests, and dirt and din. After all, hasn't the Lord shown us heavenly hospitality? Hasn't he welcomed us into his household, even though we are needy, and sometimes unpleasant, and forget to wipe our feet, and make an awful lot of noise? And won't he welcome us into far more glorious eternal dwellings when we leave our 'earthly tent' behind (*2 Cor.* 5:1)? Of course, every family needs time to itself, and we ought to care about the appearance (and volume level!) of our home, but these can easily become excuses for house-olatry.

What about you, Christian? Have you lapsed into a selfish 'moat-and-drawbridge' mentality when it comes to your house? Would a 'Beware of Homeowner' sign be appropriate on your front door? Or perhaps 'By Appointment Only'? Have you become so attached to your house that the thought you might have to leave it one day and move into another elicits an 'Over my dead body!' in your heart? If so, then you have lost sight of just how temporary is your earthly dwelling, and just how glorious—and everlasting— will be the new creation to come. You have come to treat your earthly home as if it were the only one you will ever have, or are willing to have. Conversely, the one who can say with the Apostle Paul, 'I will most gladly spend and be spent' in the service of others

(2 *Cor.* 12:15) will use his house that way: he will gladly 'spend' his house so as to receive and refresh others. He will send the signal that others are welcome in his home, and he will keep it stocked in order to be ready for them. And if in God's providence he has to move, though that may mean real challenges and sorrows (trust me, I know this from personal experience), he will also view it as a transition from one instrument for hospitality to another.

Most of us know such people and the experience of being welcomed into their homes. I vividly recall how it felt to visit the Alexandria, Virginia house where my wife's parents lived for over twenty years. When you went through the front door, it felt as if the house hugged you. (In part it felt that way because Christy's mother *did* hug you.) The family room was furnished with sofas that practically begged you to flop down on them, and to get to that room you had to pass through the kitchen where there was regularly fare for snacking ready at hand. Christy's father was always glad to build a fire in the fireplace—and Christy will be the first to admit that she regularly asked him to do so, even when the temperature outside made it questionable fire weather. (Roasted marshmallows in May, anyone?) No doubt we sometimes forgot to wipe our feet when we went in, and eventually our visits began to involve 'dirt and din' of a baby variety (that is, diapers and bawling), but we always felt welcome. Their home became something of a retreat centre for our family. And not for our family only. Time would fail me to tell of all the dinner guests, and large receptions, and weekly Bible studies. Truly, Hal and Linda Olson spent that house in the service of others. Now they have both left their earthly tents behind to enter Christ's heavenly home. Surely he will honour them in the end for having honoured him in this way.

Jonathan Edwards preached that heaven is a 'world of love'. Christy's parents' house was such a world-in-advance. In fact, there was even a plaque on the wall in their kitchen that read, 'A happy home is but an earlier heaven.' Indeed it was. May the same be said of our homes too.

3. MISERIES AND MISTREATMENT

The reality of heaven ought to make a difference in Christians' lives in times of difficulty. And since everyone experiences difficulties of various shapes and sizes daily, 'times of difficulty' amounts to 'always'.

Listen to Paul as he sizes up sufferings in Romans 8: 'For I consider that the sufferings of this present time are not worth comparing with the glory that is to be revealed to us' (verse 18). This brings to mind his words in 2 Corinthians 4 which we have already considered: 'For this light momentary affliction is preparing for us an eternal weight of glory beyond all comparison' (verse 17). 'Not worth comparing'. 'Beyond all comparison'. Size up present sufferings next to heavenly glory and suddenly the sufferings look so small that you strain to see them.

Someone might say, 'That's easy for the Apostle Paul to say. He didn't have to go through what I'm going through right now.' That is a heartfelt plea, and we dare not dismiss it. In response we need only point out what Paul *did* go through. In fact, Paul himself pointed that out. In 2 Corinthians 11 he speaks of his 'far greater labours, far more imprisonments, with countless beatings, and often near death' (verse 23). And then he goes into grim detail:

> Five times I received at the hands of the Jews the forty lashes less one. Three times I was beaten with rods. Once I was stoned. Three times I was shipwrecked; a night and a day I was adrift at sea; on frequent journeys, in danger from rivers, danger from robbers, danger from my own people, danger from Gentiles, danger in the city, danger in the wilderness, danger at sea, danger from false brothers; in toil and hardship, through many a

sleepless night, in hunger and thirst, often without food, in cold and exposure (verses 24-27).

You see, when Paul refers to 'light momentary affliction', and when he judges present sufferings 'not worth comparing' to heavenly glory, those are not the musings of an ivory tower theologian who had only read about suffering in books. After all he went through, Paul could have read stories of suffering in the marks on his own weary body. And yet still he considered earthly sufferings to be so vastly outweighed by the world to come—literally outweighed: 'an eternal *weight* of glory'—that he judged it a waste of time to bother putting them on the scales.

We all know well that when we are suffering, the temptation is to look down—down at our circumstances, down at our pain—and stay that way. It feels as if a weight has been draped over our necks, dragging our gaze down to the ground. How important it is in such moments to lift our eyes—even if we have to fight to do so. And sometimes it is a fight. We need to fix our gaze again on God, reminded that we are on our way to God ('we rejoice in hope of the glory of God'—*Rom.* 5:2). We may need the faithful words of a friend, reminding us to do just that when we have proven forgetful. In moments of solitude we may even need to hear our own words, spoken to ourselves as if into a spiritual mirror. Psalm 42:5 captures this poignantly. Listen to the Psalmist as he interrogates himself: 'Why are you cast down, O my soul, and why are you in turmoil within me?' How vivid is that description, 'cast down'. Can you not picture him, gazing to the ground, seeing nothing anymore but his own earthly despair? Thankfully he knew the solution: 'Hope in God; for I shall again praise him, my salvation.' In other words, he tells himself, 'Lift your eyes!' Look upward: look at God again. Look forward: look at your hope again. We Christians today ought to follow his lead. And whenever we do so, we know it was Christ himself who placed his strong hand under our weary chin and raised our head so that we might catch a fresh sight of his love and our hope. Then we can look back down at our pain, but now we see it in a new light, in a heavenly light. We find that, though the pain has not disappeared, somehow it looks different now. Smaller. Weaker. Shorter.

For some there is a particular kind of misery that must be endured: mistreatment at the hands of others. Peter treated this topic in his first letter:

> Servants, be subject to your masters with all respect, not only to the good and gentle but also to the unjust. For this is a gracious thing, when, mindful of God, one endures sorrows while suffering unjustly. For what credit is it if, when you sin and are beaten for it, you endure? But if when you do good and suffer for it you endure, this is a gracious thing in the sight of God (2:18-20).

Peter's words in this passage are addressed to servants, in particular, but there is a principle here that applies to all Christians: look heavenward in the midst of mistreatment. Peter refers to enduring suffering and sorrows 'mindful of God'. He does not specify what being 'mindful of God' entails, but Paul sheds light in his teaching on this same subject: 'Whatever you do, work heartily, as for the Lord and not for men, knowing that from the Lord you will receive the inheritance as your reward. You are serving the Lord Christ. For the wrongdoer will be paid back for the wrong he has done, and there is no partiality' (*Col.* 3:23-25). Paul's words help us to see that the 'mindfulness of God' that ought to be characteristic of the Christian includes the mindfulness that God will vindicate the claims of justice in the end. Abraham asked, 'Shall not the Judge of all the earth do what is just?' (*Gen.* 18:25), and of course the answer is a resounding 'Yes!' This is one of the realities that will make heaven heavenly: in the new world there will be no lingering suspicions that ultimate justice was somehow shortchanged. All in heaven will rest in this truth for all eternity: both God's justifying of those in Christ (*Rom.* 3:26), as well as his treatment of those not in Christ, was impeccable. It is this consideration, among others, that makes it possible for Christians to respond to mistreatment the way Peter is prescribing, which is responding to it with restraint and love: not striking back, not seeking vengeance, but seeking others' good, even the good of those who have wronged us. As Peter puts it later in chapter 3: 'Do not repay evil for evil or reviling for reviling, but on the contrary, bless' (*1 Pet.* 3:9). Knowing that God will prove to be a faithful judge on the last day helps Christians to respond this way. They realize how foolish and unnecessary it would be for them to try to tear the reins of justice out of God's hands. Paul makes the same point: we are never to avenge ourselves, but to trust God's justice and seek to bless instead (*Rom.* 12:19-21).

Back now to our text in 1 Peter 2, Peter goes on to remind servants—and thus all Christians—that Jesus set us an example in this regard. Immediately after urging servants to show self-restraint, Peter writes this:

> For to this you have been called, because Christ also suffered for you, leaving you an example, so that you might follow in his steps. He committed no sin, neither was deceit found in his mouth. When he was reviled, he did not revile in return; when he suffered, he did not threaten, but continued entrusting himself to him who judges justly (verses 21-23).

Notice, Jesus has left us a double example: we ought to emulate both his outward conduct and his inward disposition. What was his outward conduct? When wronged he did not strike back, but kept to his calling (in his case, a Messianic calling). What was his inward disposition? He remembered that his Father is just, and thus entrusted himself to him. While being arrested, interrogated, mocked, beaten and crucified, Jesus Christ lifted his eyes, and with his eyes on heaven he pressed on, faithful to the end.

Stop and think about a time in your life when you were wronged. Perhaps you were physically harmed. Maybe you were lied to, or lied about. Perhaps you were embarrassingly insulted before a crowd of friends or colleagues. Maybe your property was intentionally damaged. Perhaps your reputation was intentionally damaged when you were falsely found guilty of some accusation. The possibilities are many.

Here's the question: when you were wronged, how did you react? Did you strike back? You might have done so with deeds or with words, with thoughts or with emotions. 'Vengeance is mine, I will repay, says the Lord' (*Rom.* 12:19). 'No, Lord', you replied, 'it's mine. I will repay. And I will do so now. Watch me.' Perhaps you struck back with a closed fist of your own, not in self-defence but in a spirit of vengeance. Maybe you sent an email designed to damage your mistreater's reputation even worse than he just damaged yours. Perhaps you resorted to fantasy, rehearsing in your mind sinfully satisfying scenarios in which the one who wronged you got his comeuppance. Maybe you nursed hatred in your heart. I suspect that few remember the 1984 film *Red Dawn*, but I certainly remember this exchange between one character and a young man left embittered by wrongs done to him: 'All that hate's gonna burn you up, kid.' His answer? 'It keeps me warm.'

Thus there are so many forms, outward and inward, that retaliation might take. That time when you were wronged, did you strike back? If you did, the explanation, at least in part, is certainly this: you took your mind off things above. You closed your heart-eyes to heaven. Instead of being mindful of God and of his determination to satisfy the claims of justice at the end of the age, you allowed yourself to become selfishly absorbed with the here-and-now, especially your own pain. And that led you to want to make pain for your enemy in return.

Whenever you have retaliated like that, it is time to look upward, look forward, and repent. Look upward to God in heaven, for he is just. Look forward to the day when his justice will be manifested, for that day is coming. Just like Jesus, entrust yourself to him who judges justly.

This also applies to circumstances in which we are not the one wronged, but we are aware of wrong done to others. Have you ever seen news footage of a scene in which a person who has been found guilty—or who is merely suspected—of having committed some ghastly crime is ushered into the courthouse, or perhaps into prison, past a crowd of violently angry onlookers? Those are chilling scenes. And they are chilling, not just because of the crime that was committed, but also because of the shouts and signs and faces of some of the onlookers. If you have ever seen such footage then you can imagine them. Their eyes are practically blood-red with rage, and their words are too. They cry out for punishments that make 'cruel and unusual' sound mild.

What has led to this? What explains such reactions? There are many answers to that question. One answer is this: what has led to such scenes is blindness to the scene in heaven, where the Judge of all the earth sits enthroned in glory and his Messianic Son has been installed at his right hand, both of them committed to the cause of justice, the Son uniquely destined to return to earth and vindicate that cause in the end. Block out that scene, and at that point the infliction of earthly pains is the only 'justice' that remains. And so the angry onlookers cry out for punishments they think will exceed the crime. And yet their cries are only made all the more desperate by the unshakable realization that no earthly pains can possibly make up for the devastation that sorrowing loved ones have known, and thus bring about justice for the crime committed.

What is the answer? The answer is, lift your eyes. Behold again that heavenly scene, where Justice dwells, whence justice shall swiftly descend. When you have done so, when you have taken these truths to heart, you will still feel anger about earthly crimes. You ought to. And you will still pray for the proper functioning of earthly courts. We need them. But you will also feel self-control, and show it. For you will have been reminded that there is a higher court, and an ultimate justice. And as a Christian you will also have been reminded that you yourself are a sinner who has been forgiven, and thus made ready for final judgment, thanks to immeasurable mercy. He has not dealt with you according to your sins, nor repaid you according to your iniquities (*Psa.* 103:10). Come to grips with that, and you will leave the courthouse sidewalk, go home, tear up your sign, kneel down, look up to heaven, and pray.

CONCLUSION

In this chapter, we have turned our attention to marriage; money and moving; and miseries and mistreatment. Of course this is just a sampler. There are many other areas of life that the hope of heaven rightly transforms. In fact, it ought to impact them all. Hopefully our survey of these subjects has been enough to show that heavenly-mindedness pays off. Hopefully by now we can all agree, this is the way to be!

But if this is such a God-glorifying, Christ-honouring, life-enriching way to live, why do we often find heavenly-mindedness to be in short supply? Good question. Turn the page to Part 2 and let's start answering it.

Unless, of course, you want to place your bookmark here and go for a walk and reflect. Remember, I'm all for that.

Part 2:
The Cure for What Ails Us

Is there such a rest remaining for us? Why, then, are our thoughts no more upon it? Why are not our hearts continually there? Why dwell we not there in constant contemplation? What is the cause of this neglect?

RICHARD BAXTER
The Saints' Everlasting Rest

IN the Introduction I noted the calling to be heavenly-minded, and then I asked, 'Why aren't we? Why do we find it so hard to live steadfastly heaven-directed, heaven-saturated lives?' Here in Part 2 we will address that question head-on.

Sit down with a pen and paper and write down the reasons that come to mind for our lack of heavenly-mindedness, and you can come up with quite a list. In these pages we will consider various factors that tend to push heaven out of our minds, as well as truths we can embrace, and steps we can take, to push it back to where it belongs.

Come, let us regain our heavenly bearings together.

CHAPTER FIVE

Mourning into Dancing

We neglect to set our minds on heaven . . .
Because of despair over the prospect of our making it in.
So let us grasp again the gospel of free, almighty grace.

IT sounds like something out of a Jane Austen novel. Imagine
this fictional storyline. Two young women, dear friends since
childhood, have both received invitations to a much-anticipated
ball to take place at an opulent manor house. In fact, not only has
the host of the ball extended invitations to the young ladies, he has
also promised to send his own private carriage to their homes that
evening to whisk them to the occasion in luxury and security.

As our next scene opens, soon after the invitations have arrived,
the two young women are walking together and talking with each
other about all these things that have happened. It becomes clear
even from the manner of their walking that they are in two very
different frames of mind. The one is practically skipping for joy
over the invitation, the other is plodding slowly, eyes cast down.
What has made the difference?

Young Woman #1 inquires, 'Friend, tell me, why so troubled?
Do we not have great cause for joy? We have received invitations
from the host of the ball! It must be that he desires our presence
there! And so desirous is he that he has even promised to dispatch
his own carriage to get us there! Why then this long face and this
sorrowful gait?'

Young Woman #2 replies, 'Speak to me no more of this ball, for I now find the very thought of it distressing to my soul. Yes, the host has promised us his carriage, but how can we know it will actually come for us? Perhaps we will prepare ourselves for the evening, only to find that the carriage never arrives, and thus that we are never taken. Or perhaps the carriage will come for us, but we will find our route blocked by some obstacle along the way, so that we are forced to return home. And even if we do finally arrive at the manor, how can I be sure I will be welcomed there? How can I know the host will not have changed in his disposition toward me, and I find myself, in spite of this invitation, finally turned away in shame?'

Her friend listens patiently, although she marvels at the sound of these suspicions. She seeks to lift her friend's spirits by all manner of arguments, but her efforts prove futile. Try as she might, her melancholy companion remains unmoved. These doubts simply will not let her go. Instead of *Sense and Sensibility,* we will entitle our story, *Delight and Despair.*

Notice that our Young Woman #2 is plagued by double despair: she doubts that she will arrive at the ball, plus she doubts, even if she does arrive, that she will be welcomed. Sadly, some Christians suffer from similar discouragements with respect to their place in heaven. 'What if I don't make it there? What if I give up in this life along the way?', they wonder. 'And even if I do make it there, how can I know I won't be turned away at the door because I wasn't good enough to get in?' Those who live with such oppressive spiritual burdens weighing them down are almost certain not to be heavenly-minded, because the very thought of heaven only makes them miserable. Who would take time to set his mind on the world above when he cannot get past the suspicion that, in the end, he will have no place in that world? Who would go out of her way to day-dream about a ball when she simply cannot bring herself to believe that she will be there, joining in the laughing and dancing and feasting? Doubts about arriving, plus doubts about acceptance: let us give each of these due consideration.

1. What if I don't make it there?

The issue before us here is that of the perseverance of believers. Jesus said, 'the one who endures to the end will be saved' (*Matt.* 24:13). Paul told the Colossians they could look forward to being presented holy to God 'if indeed you continue in the faith, stable and steadfast, not shifting from the hope of the gospel that you heard' (*Col.* 1:23). Clearly, Jesus' disciples must persevere as disciples, pressing on in faith, hope and love, and they will only 'gain the everlasting hall' if they do so. Unfortunately, some believers harbour the fear they will not persevere and reach heaven. 'Sure, I believe in Christ now', they say, 'but how can I know I'll believe in him tomorrow, and the next day, and all my days? How can I know I won't bail out at some point along the way?'

The answer is, he can know he will persevere because God has promised to bring that about. Paul pronounced this benediction over the Thessalonians: 'Now may the God of peace himself sanctify you completely, and may your whole spirit and soul and body be kept blameless at the coming of our Lord Jesus Christ. He who calls you is faithful; he will surely do it' (*1 Thess.* 5:23-24). You see, for Paul it was a matter of divine faithfulness that those who begin in Christ keep going and reach the end. Put negatively, it would amount to divine faithlessness—that is, God would have broken his promise—if anyone who comes to faith in Christ bails out on him completely some time later. Remember our discussion of the new birth in Chapter 2: the same God who powerfully brought the sinner to new life in the first place will also powerfully sustain that new life once he has created it. Thus is the believer preserved in faith and in the love by which faith is manifested ('faith working through love'—*Gal.* 5:6).

To reinforce this point, listen to Paul's words at the dramatic climax of Romans 8: 'For I am sure that neither death nor life, nor angels nor rulers, nor things present nor things to come, nor powers, nor height nor depth, nor anything else in all creation, will be able to separate us from the love of God in Christ Jesus our Lord' (verses 38-39). Do you see how sweeping is Paul's declaration? That passage comes crashing pitifully to the ground, and the whole gospel with it, if we carve out some kind of exception: 'Yes, but that doesn't mean the believer can't turn traitor and thus finally separate *himself* from God.' Come now! If that were possible, Paul's words are simply silly. In that passage he would be canvassing the entire created order from top to bottom, ruling out anything and everything that might take us away from God, all the while overlooking the one enemy closest to home: our own sinful nature. Such a suggestion makes a mockery of the apostle's ringing affirmation and guts it of its hope-giving power. No, Paul must mean that nothing—absolutely nothing—can take us away from God, thus ruling out a treacherous about-face on our part by which we revert to utter unbelief. Paul must mean that the Christian will keep going after all.

In a sermon entitled 'Foretastes of the Heavenly Life', nineteenth-century London preacher C. H. Spurgeon made this point powerfully. Spurgeon earnestly loved to preach the gospel: 'Tell me the day I do not preach, I will tell you the day in which I am not happy.'[1] Thus it is jarring to hear Spurgeon say that any consideration could have caused him to 'renounce the pulpit'. What prospect provoked such strong language from him? It was, he explained, the prospect of preaching the gospel without the liberty to preach the doctrine of the perseverance of believers. Deny that doctrine, he said, and preaching proves pointless and the gospel is gutted of good news. Here's how he put it:

[1] Charles Spurgeon, 'Foretastes of the Heavenly Life', in *Spurgeon's Sermons*, vol. 3 (Grand Rapids, Michigan: Baker, 2004), p. 142.

O how I love that doctrine of the perseverance of the saints. I renounce the pulpit when I can not preach it, for the gospel seems to be a blank desert and a howling wilderness—a gospel as unworthy of God as it would be beneath even my acceptance, frail worm as I am—a gospel which saves me to-day and rejects me to-morrow—a gospel which puts me in Christ's family one hour, and makes me a child of the devil the next—a gospel which justifies and then condemns me—a gospel which pardons me, and afterward casts me to hell. Such a gospel is abhorrent to reason itself, much more to the God of the whole earth. But on the other ground of faith, that 'He to the end must endure, As sure as the earnest is given',[2] we do enjoy a sense of perfect security even as we dwell in this land of wars and fightings.[3]

Once again, Spurgeon the master preacher hit the nail on the head. The Bible's teaching that believers endure as believers gives preaching purpose and gives Christians confidence. In short, it makes the good news truly, thoroughly good.

Two key clarifications are in order. First, the person who perseveres in faith is the *genuine* believer, emphasis on 'genuine'. It must be acknowledged that some claim to believe in Christ whose faith is something other than the real deal. They have aligned themselves with Christ's cause for some other reason than a genuine commitment to him. The Lord himself confronted this during his earthly ministry: some who claimed to believe in him eventually turned their backs on him, even betraying him (*John* 6:64). The Apostle John recognized this too: he spoke of those who align themselves with the church and then depart ('They went out from us'), thus betraying that they had never truly belonged to the church with a sincere faith in the first place ('they were not of us'—*1 John* 2:19).

---

[2] Here Spurgeon is alluding to the language of Augustus Toplady's hymn, 'A Debtor to Mercy Alone'.

[3] Spurgeon, 'Foretastes', p. 140.

There is no denying that some who profess faith in Christ later turn their backs on him, never returning, but by that desertion they only manifest that theirs was never saving faith. It is sobering to say so, but biblical. But the one who finds genuine faith within need not paralyze himself with fears about his own perseverance. He will certainly persevere, because the Lord will certainly preserve him.

Second, as we noted back in Chapter 2, even the genuine believer sins regularly, and sometimes grievously. He may even fall deeply into rebellion and stay there for a season. David stands out in Scripture as a clear example of this (adultery, followed by murder, followed by months before the prophet Nathan brought him back to his spiritual senses; see *2 Sam.* 11-12). And yet even during such personal 'dark ages' in the life of the believer there is a seed of life and faith that survives, for there is the sealing ministry of the Holy Spirit preserving that seed (*Eph.* 1:13-14). And thus there is the certainty that in due time—that is, in God's good time, which to us may seem a long time—the believer so weakened will gain strength again and rise up renewed in the service of the Lord.

2. Even if I do make it there, how can I know I won't be turned away at the door because I wasn't good enough to get in?

The popular image here is that of Peter (usually denominated 'St Peter' in these stories) presiding at the so-called 'pearly gates' of heaven, interrogating the soul of every human being who has just died and then rendering his verdict: either the person did sufficient good on earth to be admitted to heaven, or he failed to do so and is thus summarily dispatched to hell (or at least politely turned away from heaven, since the notion of 'hell' may be deemed unacceptable). A popular image? Yes. A biblical image? Not at all! In fact, nearly the only biblical thing about it is that there once was a man named Peter and, yes, Peter is now in heaven. That much is true. But this conception of heavenly judgment is most untrue.

At the heart of the gospel is this: we do not gain a title to heaven because our good works were good enough to earn it, but because Christ was good enough to gain it for us, and our faith is in him. He loved his Father with unblemished holiness in thought, word and deed ('in every respect . . . tempted as we are, yet without sin'—*Heb.* 4:15), and then he laid down his life to suffer the curse that we deserved ('Christ redeemed us from the curse of the law by becoming a curse for us'—*Gal.* 3:13). He who thus lived and died now lives in heaven, and those who trust in him to save them and not in their own moral performance can be assured they will gain admission and join him when they die. Paul could hardly make it any clearer than he does in Galatians 2:16: 'we know that a person is not justified by works of the law but through faith in Jesus Christ, so we also have believed in Christ Jesus, in order to be justified by faith in Christ and not by works of the law, because by works of the law no one will be justified.' Good news: that justification policy will be just as true when you die as it is now when you live; and it will be just as true on the day Jesus returns to judge the world as it was every day prior. You will not arrive at the gates of heaven (if we can even speak of 'gates') only to find that the terms of peace are different from those offered and accepted when you first believed.

Yes, when the believer is admitted into the holy fellowship of heaven he will have been completely sanctified, purged of all remaining sin. Remember, he will have taken his place among 'the spirits of the righteous made perfect' (*Heb.* 12:23). But his personal holiness will not be regarded as the meritorious ground of his being admitted. Rather, the Lord by his grace will have completed the believer's sanctification at death to make it possible for him to step into the presence of God. His gracious justification entitles him to heaven, and the completion of his gracious sanctification fits him for it. So too, in the last judgment at the end of the age the Lord will acknowledge the good works his people performed during this life. Then will the Son of Man distinguish the sheep from the goats according to their treatment of those who belonged to him (*Matt.* 25:31-45). But the good works of his people will not be acknowledged as having earned them heaven. Rather, their works will be publicly recognized on that day as the faith-evidencing reality they were all along. Thus in the end will the holiness of God be manifested, and his gracious ways vindicated.

So, do you worry that you will be turned away from heaven because your good works were not quite good enough? Hear the verdict: your good works aren't good enough to earn you a place in heaven, they never were, and they never will be. The question is not, are you good enough?, but, was Jesus good enough? Was his life of righteousness, culminating in his death on the cross, good enough to gain you a place in the kingdom? Of course it was! And of course the Father knows it was, and will honour it accordingly. So then, the question is, do you trust in Jesus to be such a Saviour to you? Do you?

Here let us revisit the prophet Isaiah and his vision of the heavenly throne room. His exposure to the holiness of God drives him to exclaim:

> 'Woe is me! For I am lost; for I am a man of unclean lips, and I dwell in the midst of a people of unclean lips; for my eyes have seen the King, the LORD of hosts!' Then one of the seraphim flew to me, having in his hand a burning coal that he had taken with tongs from the altar. And he touched my mouth and said: 'Behold, this has touched your lips; your guilt is taken away, and your sin atoned for.' And I heard the voice of the Lord saying, 'Whom shall I send, and who will go for us?' Then I said, 'Here am I! Send me' (*Isa.* 6:5-8).

How different is Isaiah's outlook at the end of the passage compared to his condition at the beginning: from 'Woe is me!' to 'Send me.' What made the difference? Did Isaiah summon his courage and manage to make a persuasive case before the bar of divine judgment that his personal holiness was sufficient to earn a pass? No, not at all. What made the difference was atonement and forgiveness. He was made fit for the judgment of God, not by his own works, but by the work of God to provide for his needs. So may the Christian look forward to his reception into heaven at death, and on the last day: he knows that in Christ God has made full provision for his justification, and that by faith alone he has savingly availed himself of that provision. He will certainly not be turned away, for the Father will certainly not fail to honour the redeeming work of the Son.

DOUBLY KEPT

What have we seen thus far? (1) The believer who harbours doubts about his arriving at the door of heaven needs a dose of the doctrine of perseverance. (2) The believer who wonders if he will be welcomed through the door of heaven needs to revisit the doctrine of justification. There is good news—*great news!*—on both fronts. (1) It is our almighty God who preserves. (2) It is our steadfast God who welcomes.

See how these two themes come together in the opening of Peter's First Letter. Peter begins with praise: 'Blessed be the God and Father of our Lord Jesus Christ!' (*1 Pet.* 1:3). What has inspired this doxology? Peter explains:

the God and Father of our Lord Jesus Christ . . . has caused us to be born again to a living hope through the resurrection of Jesus Christ from the dead, to an inheritance that is imperishable, undefiled, and unfading, kept in heaven for you, who by God's power are being guarded through faith for a salvation ready to be revealed in the last time (verses 3-5).

Notice, first, Christians 'are being guarded . . . by God's power'.

> A mighty fortress is our God,
> A bulwark never failing.[4]

The Father protects his children. No, he does not protect them from all earthly ills. But he does protect them in the way that matters most: he sees to it that the Evil One and all other evil influences do not completely sever his children's connection to Christ.

Notice, second, our inheritance is being 'kept in heaven' for us. And what an inheritance! 'Imperishable, undefiled, and unfading'. Peter is using figurative language here: he speaks of our inheritance as if it were an *it*—a *thing* that God is keeping safe for us and will one day present to us—when in reality our inheritance is a *he*. That is, our inheritance is nothing other than knowing God himself in the way that the residents of heaven know him now and will do so forever. Do you think the God and Father of our Lord Jesus Christ is the kind of father who would promise such an inheritance to his children only to renege later? By no means! As Paul reminded the Ephesians, upon coming to faith believers are 'sealed with the promised Holy Spirit, who is the guarantee of our inheritance until we acquire possession of it, to the praise of his glory' (*Eph.* 1:13-14). You see, the gift of the Spirit is God's guarantee that we will eventually come into the fulness of our inheritance, for the Spirit himself is nothing less than a divine downpayment on that inheritance. In the ministry of the Spirit, we enjoy on earth a first portion of the life of heaven. The remainder must eventually follow, for our God honours his downpayments.

Now, see how those two points that Peter makes answer the two doubts with which we began this chapter. Like Young Woman

[4] Words by Martin Luther, 1529. Translated by Frederick H. Hedge, 1853.

#2 in our dramatic tale, the Christian may be plagued by double despair: (1) Will I arrive? and (2) Will I be welcomed? Here in 1 Peter 1 both of those doubts are answered, for our God is a Double Keeper: (1) *We* are kept, and (2) *Our inheritance* is kept. We will not fall away along the way, nor will we be turned away at the door. Throughout this life we are guarded by God's power, and then at the end of this life we will come into the full possession of the inheritance that has been waiting for us all along.

THE END

Not every novel has a happy ending (not every novel should), but *Delight and Despair* does. Imagine the look on the face of our Young Woman #2 when she alights from the carriage and steps tentatively toward the entrance to the manor . . . only to find that the host is already stepping toward her and her friend, beaming, glad for their presence, eager to welcome them. She has arrived, and she has been accepted. Young Woman #1, a playful friend, whispers 'I told you so', but it has no malice in it. Despair is no more, only shared delight. The promise was kept, and the invitation was honoured. Let the music begin!

Christian, the gospel of Jesus Christ—more precisely, your personal part in the gospel story—will have the most satisfying of happy endings. Do you doubt it? Put those doubts to rest once and for all. The promise of your safe conduct was made by God, and all his promises are kept. The invitation in your hands was sent from God, and he will not change his mind. Take heart: you will arrive at the feast, and you will be welcomed by the host, and once welcomed you will never be sent away. So think on heaven, and rejoice. Again I will say, Rejoice!

CHAPTER SIX

Face Forward

We neglect to set our minds on heaven . . .
Because of difficulty coming to grips with the past.
So let us learn to see the past in the light of the future.

YOU have likely heard someone referred to as a 'hopeless romantic'. But have you ever heard someone described as a 'hopeless nostalgic'?

I suppose that charge might be levelled against me. Mine was a sweet childhood lived in a loving family. For that reason I find it both satisfying and fascinating whenever we visit the place where I grew up and memories of those years come to mind. Now, with children of my own, I feel the same way about remembering their earlier years. Seeing a photograph, watching a home video, hearing a certain song, revisiting a significant site—all these have the power to take me back, and I, for one, regularly enjoy the ride. I see no need to take detours in order to avoid Memory Lane.

Then again, to say that I am a 'hopeless' nostalgic is putting it too strongly. After all, I do not *live* on Memory Lane. I only pass that way every once in a while. I live in the present, with all its blessings and banes, and I look forward to the future from here. For some people, however, when it comes to their relationship to the past, the adjective 'hopeless' is all too fitting. It is said of them that they are 'living in the past'. For example, some remember a season in their own life when all seemed to be well—an idyllic season long since past, for emptiness now prevails. For the Christian that may be the memory of a high point in his spiritual past, a time when he seemed to know God with an intimacy that he no longer enjoys. Some look all the way back to what appears in the history books to have been a better age for the church or society as a whole. Some remember loved ones who have died, recalling the joy of knowing them, and then the profound sorrow of losing them. Some remember vividly their own past sins. Some remain wounded by great wrongs that others committed against them. We all carry with us memories like these, whether bitter or sweet, but some people, unfortunately, are obsessed with them. The past dominates their thinking. It consumes their energies. It determines their mood. It defines who they are. They are stuck trying to recreate the past, or to erase it, or to avenge it, or to deaden their hearts so that they no longer feel anything about it. They may even find themselves torn, feeling drawn to the past one day and then haunted by it the next.

If this is true of you, it is not hard to imagine what this means for heavenly-mindedness. In short, it means you won't be. After all, your fundamental orientation can be either looking backward or looking forward. It cannot be both. Picture your posture on the timeline of your own life: turn and face the past as one obsessed with it, and see that you have thereby turned your back on the future. You have put the future—heaven included—largely out of sight and out of mind. Thus the adjective 'hopeless' fits. It fits for two reasons. First, all your strenuous past-directed efforts will prove futile. Try to recreate the past, and the outcome will not quite live up to what you remember. Try to erase the past, and even if you succeed, more or less, at blocking out a particular memory, you will never know deep resolution and peace. Try to avenge the past, and the vengeance will not taste quite as sweet as you imagined it would. Try to deaden yourself against the past, and you will be trying to become something less than human, for to be human is to be one who feels. You see, those are dead ends, all of them. Second, the adjective 'hopeless' fits because all the time you spend obsessed with the past is time not spent rejoicing in and longing for the world to come. This is no way to live. It is an enslaving way to live. It is time to be set free.

PAUL'S PAST

There are valuable lessons to be learned from the Apostle Paul about how rightly to relate to the past, including our personal past. Consider his testimony in Philippians 3. Having spoken of his determination to participate in the resurrection from the dead, Paul goes on to say this:

> Not that I have already obtained this or am already perfect, but I press on to make it my own, because Christ Jesus has made me his own. Brothers, I do not consider that I have made it my own. But one thing I do: forgetting what lies behind and straining forward to what lies ahead, I press on toward the goal for the prize of the upward call of God in Christ Jesus (verses 12-14).

See how Paul related to the past: 'forgetting what lies behind'.

Now, did Paul really forget what lay behind him? I mean, did he do so in the sense of achieving actual amnesia with respect to his past life, including his past sins? Not at all. In fact he describes his past life, including some of his past sins, in the verses just prior to these in Philippians 3! He refers to his previous sense of self-identity in these terms: 'circumcised on the eighth day, of the people of Israel, of the tribe of Benjamin, a Hebrew of Hebrews; as to the law, a Pharisee; as to zeal, a persecutor of the church; as to righteousness under the law, blameless' (verses 5-6). Paul remembered a great deal about his past life, and he was willing to put it in writing.

Not only so, but looking beyond this one chapter in Philippians to the rest of the New Testament, we see that Paul was eager to tell the old, old story of his pre-Christian life over and over again. He tells his story in Acts 22 before the crowd in Jerusalem, and then again in Acts 26 before King Agrippa in Cæsarea. He tells his story to the Galatians in the first two chapters of that letter. In 1 Timothy he puts it plainly: 'I thank him who has given me strength, Christ Jesus our Lord, because he judged me faithful, appointing me to his service, though formerly I was a blasphemer, persecutor, and insolent opponent' (*1 Tim.* 1:12-13). He then goes on to sum up the gospel in these personal terms:

> The saying is trustworthy and deserving of full acceptance, that Christ Jesus came into the world to save sinners, of whom I am the foremost. But I received mercy for this reason, that in me, as the foremost, Jesus Christ might display his perfect patience as an example to those who were to believe in him for eternal life (verses 15-16).

You see, Paul remembered that he had been a fierce opponent of Christ and of his people. From these passages it becomes clear: for Paul 'forgetting what lies behind' did not mean erasing his past from his personal memory bank.

To be clear, the lesson to be learned here is not that the Christian must regularly recount to others tales of his former sins. There are moments in which such revelations may be called for—in the context of his unique apostolic calling Paul knew what those moments were, and what was right to say—but those moments are relatively rare. Especially in the case of past *private* sins, known only to the sinner and God, those moments are rare. Such revelations are often self-serving and scandalizing instead of edifying. In this tell-all, talk show culture in which we live, we are prone to reveal far more than is prudent. The lesson to be learned is simply this: our duty with respect to the past is not to eliminate it from our minds. Paul's example teaches us this.

Not only did Paul remember his own past sins, but sometimes he even reminded other Christians of their past sins too. For example, Paul urged the Colossians to put to death things like 'sexual immorality, impurity, passion, evil desire, and covetousness, which is idolatry (*Col.* 3:5). A few verses later he adds 'anger, wrath, malice, slander, and obscene talk from your mouth' (verse 8). And in between he says this: 'In these you too once walked, when you were living in them' (verse 7). This proves the same point: Christian faithfulness does not entail trying to erase memories, even painful ones.

But if this is true—if by 'forgetting what lies behind' in Philippians 3 Paul does not mean achieving actual amnesia—the question remains, what does he mean? So far in our interpretation we have only ruled out a wrong turn . . . but which is the right one? The answer lies in what Paul goes on to say: 'forgetting what lies behind and *straining forward to what lies ahead, I press on toward the goal for the prize of the upward call of God in Christ Jesus*' (verses 13-14). You see, Paul 'forgot' what lay behind him in the sense that he resolutely refused to allow concern with the past to become his defining orientation. He was determined that the past would not shackle him. He would gain his sense of identity from the future, and set his affections on it, and direct his energies toward it. For Paul this meant gaining his identity from *Christ,* and setting his affections on Christ, and directing his energies toward Christ, because for the Christian Christ is the future. There can only be one all-consuming reality in any person's life. Paul resolved, 'In my life that reality will not be my past but my future.' He had two choices: he could face what lay behind, obsessed with it, mourning over old sins without new joy, or he could turn and face the future and run toward it, even strive toward it, with every ounce of his being. He chose the latter. He strained forward. He pressed on. And all the while he remembered what he used to be, and he rejoiced and gave thanks to God that he wasn't that anymore.

Ironically, Paul was able to press on like that, fixed on the future, precisely because his life was founded upon events that took place in the past! I mean these: the death and resurrection of the Lord Jesus Christ, with his lowly birth and life beforehand, and his glorious ascension and outpouring of the Spirit afterward. The saving acts of God in Christ occupied the centre of Paul's outlook, shaping the way he thought, prayed and lived, and the same should be true of us today, nearly two thousand years later. How frequently in Scripture we come across the calling to remember. The summons has always been, 'Remember what God has done.' For God's Old Covenant people, that meant remembering their deliverance from Egypt in order to inherit the land of the Canaanites. 'You shall remember that you were a slave in the land of Egypt, and the LORD your God redeemed you' (*Deut.* 15:15). For us, God's New Covenant people, that means remembering the works of God in Christ, chiefly his atoning death and his victorious resurrection. 'Remember Jesus Christ, risen from the dead, the offspring of David' (*2 Tim.* 2:8). Under the Old Covenant the Lord provided memorials, like the institution of the Passover, to serve as reminders of what he had done for his people. Concerning the Passover the Lord said, 'This day shall be for you a memorial day, and you shall keep it as a feast to the LORD; throughout your generations, as a statute forever, you shall keep it as a feast' (*Exod.* 12:14). Under the New Covenant God has made the same sort of provision: whenever the Lord's Supper is administered we 'proclaim the Lord's death until he comes' (*1 Cor.* 11:26).

So, does this mean that the Christian lives in the past after all? No, for even the works of God in Christ all those years ago have future-pointing arrows inscribed upon them. Whenever the

Christian revisits the death and resurrection of Jesus Christ (which he regularly ought to do), lo and behold, what does he find at the tomb of Jesus, but there is a footpath that begins there—a pilgrim's footpath—that leads right back into the future, all the way to the eternal future of the people of God. In his meditations the Christian goes back to the saving works of God in Jesus Christ time and time again, only to find that a proper contemplation of those works eventually redirects his gaze from past to future. Remember, Jesus lived and died and rose not simply to live and die and rise—not simply to give us something remarkable to remember—but to bring about a most glorious future. Lose sight of that, and you have lost sight of the whole point of the gospel. Consider: even the memorials God has provided point forward. The Passover feast pointed forward to the coming of the Lamb of God, who would take away the sin of the world (*John* 1:29). And now whenever the Lord's Supper is administered we proclaim the Lord's death 'until he comes'. He will come. He will come for us. And so, just like Paul, we press on until that day.

DEALING WITH OUR MEMORIES

It is this future-directed, Christ-centred outlook—and only this outlook, by the way—that finally equips Christians properly to deal with their past. For example, do you have sweet memories of growing up? Or do you remember a spiritual high point in your walk with Christ from which you have since descended? Or have you read about a season in church history when the church was stronger in some respect than it is today? Then give thanks to God for those times past. But then don't forget to keep going into the future! That means, among other things, noting the lessons rightly learned from those past seasons and then applying those lessons as you press on. They could be lessons about wise earthly living, or about fruitfulness in the Christian life, or about faithfulness on the part of the church as a whole. Look back, learn, and then march on with what you have learned. Remember, no matter how wonderful that moment in the past may have been, whether personal or historical, God has something far greater in store: nothing less than the ushering in of a glorious, eternal world for all his children. Not only so, but as you seek to grow in the grace and knowledge of our Lord Jesus Christ, God will indelibly forge the future in your own life, remaking you after Christ's image. So by all means, flip through photo albums—whether actual photo albums on your bookshelves or collections of pleasant memories stored up in your mind—but don't flip through them with the emptiness of one who thinks the past is all he has. Those in Christ have the future. The 'good old days' may have been good, but our heavenly days will be better by far. The Christian can say it like no one else can say it: 'The best is yet to come.'

On the other hand, are you haunted by the memory of your own sins? If so, the first and crucial step is this: go to God, trusting in Christ, and ask God for forgiveness if you have never done so. And then trust that he truly does forgive those who, with broken and contrite hearts, confess their sins all the while looking to the Lamb of God. 'If we confess our sins, he is faithful and just to forgive us our sins and to cleanse us from all unrighteousness' (*1 John* 1:9). That means, among other things, that you need not keep going back to God, confessing the same past sins and asking for forgiveness for them over and over again. In light of 1 John 1:9 which we just noted, to do so is to charge that God is unjust, for you thereby imply that God failed to regard the atoning work of his Son as truly effectual the first time you confessed. No, when God forgives, he means it. His forgiveness stands. It stands forever. In other words, when we confess and God forgives, it is God who has done the erasing: no, he has not erased the *fact* of our sin from history, but he has erased the *debt* that once stood between us and him on account of our sin, and when he has done so no one can rewrite it. Even God himself, for all eternity, because of his just regard for the work of his Son, will never rewrite the indictment, find us guilty, and cast us out. The Christian who struggles with the memory of his past sins does not need to learn to 'forgive himself'. People sometimes put it that way, but the very idea of forgiveness entails two parties to the transaction. There is no such thing as forgiving yourself. No, the Christian's need is to trust that God has forgiven him, and to see himself accordingly. Do you struggle to do so? Then take that very struggle to Christ too! Pray, 'I believe; help my unbelief!' (*Mark* 9:24).

In Jeremiah 31:34, God says, 'I will forgive their iniquity, and I will remember their sin no more.' *I will remember their sin no more?* If Paul's 'forgetting' did not mean achieving amnesia with respect to the past, how much less is that true of God! Do you think that divine forgiveness means God ceases to know that you did what you did? Think again. God will forever remain the all-knowing God that he has always been. For all eternity he will know all about all of your sins . . . and yet he will never retract the forgiveness he granted you in Christ Jesus when you first came to him. In that sense, God will never 'remember'.

No, this does not mean that in this life the memory of your past sins will no longer be bitter to you. It will be bitter, and, frankly, it ought to be. After all, forgiveness does not mean that your sin wasn't sin—forgiveness means it *was*—or that your sin wasn't deathly and damaging. Remember, this consideration is rightly held before young people—and not-so-young people too—as a deterrent to sin (see the book of Proverbs), and it does not cease to be true afterward. Sin makes for misery. But for the Christian the good news is this: in Christ you will have come to know a sweetness—the sweetness of new forgiveness—that trumps the bitterness of old sin. Plus yours will be the hope of a heavenly day when the bitter will be no more. 'Blessed are those who mourn, for they shall be comforted' (*Matt.* 5:4). Yes, the Christian mourns over sin, but he does not do so as others do who have no hope. He regards his past sins as past *forgiven* sins, plus he looks forward to the unblemished, uninterrupted joy of heaven, where there will be no mourning at all (*Rev.* 21:4).

Also, as it was with past blessings, so it is with past sins: there are lessons to be learned from them and taken into the future. Consider the testimony of the *Westminster Confession of Faith*. In the chapter on God's providence there is this sobering and realistic admission: 'The most wise, righteous, and gracious God doth oftentimes leave, for a season, his own children to manifold temptations, and the corruption of their own hearts' (*WCF* 5.4). In other words, in his mysterious sovereign workings God often leaves his own children to sin. Now the question is, why would he do that? Why would a 'wise, righteous and gracious God' actually allow his own beloved children to wander into sin and thereby make misery for themselves and others? Good question. The *Confession* goes on to provide a few answers. God's good purposes include these:

> to chastise them for their former sins, or to discover unto them the hidden strength of corruption and deceitfulness of their hearts, that they may be humbled; and, to raise them to a more close and constant dependence for their support upon himself, and to make them more watchful against all future occasions of sin, and for sundry other just and holy ends.

Don't you love that language at the end? 'For sundry other just and holy ends'. In other words, 'We could go on, but that's enough for now!' The point is this: the Christian can make good use of his past sins as he strives for future holiness. If nothing else, learn from your past about the power of sin, walk humbly before God and others as one over whom that power has at times prevailed, walk closely with God because you have learned the hard way that you dare not wander from him, and keep open a watchful eye to steer clear of repeating the past. In that spirit, march on. Isaac Barrow observed, 'Piety hath a wondrous virtue to change all things into matter of consolation and joy. No condition in effect can be evil or sad to a pious man', including this: 'his very sins (as breeding contrition, humility, circumspection, and vigilance), do better and profit him.'[1] So it is with the pious man, and so it is with the heavenly-minded man, for they are one and the same.

Have you ever received an invitation that requested you to RSVP, and the request was noted 'Regrets only'? Christian, do not let that be your legacy: 'Regrets only. Regrets are all he had. He never got past wishing he could go back and undo his sins. He never really repented. He never strained forward. He never pressed on. Regrets only.' No, let our lives be summarized 'Grace only' instead. Grace which forgives. Grace which transforms. Grace which points us forward.

Many of these same lessons can be brought to bear upon memories of profound sorrows we have known. Perhaps some singular event in your own life comes to mind. No, the day will never come when that sorrowful event is erased from your past, and in this life—this life of grief—the day will never come when the memory of that event does not provoke some measure of sadness. But in Christ even our grieving is transformed. Counselling the Christians in Thessalonica concerning the death of fellow believers, Paul wrote this: 'But we do not want you to be uninformed, brothers, about those who are asleep, that you may not grieve as others do who have no hope' (*1 Thess.* 4:13). That counsel applies broadly to sorrows of all sorts, not just the death of fellow Christians. The believer's grief over past losses is real, but it is not hopeless. Ours is

[1] As cited by C. H. Spurgeon, *The Treasury of David, vol. 3, Psalms 111-150* (Grand Rapids, Michigan: Zondervan, 1976), p. 283.

the hope of heaven, even the wiping away of every last tear, and the satisfying of every need, and the righting of every wrong.

It is this consideration that helps the Christian to rise up and carry on after some great sorrow. The one who has set his mind on the world to come finds a Spirit-wrought strength within to press on. Though he remembers what happened, and the memory of it still pains him, in due time he slowly gets back to life—back to work and relationships and interests—now forged by what happened. And over time his grief evolves. Years later his grief is not what it was in the immediate aftermath. The initial incessant searing pain has given way to a steady dull ache, perhaps with occasional piercing pangs. At first he may have been nearly doubled over, incapable of tending to basic responsibilities. Years later he is largely back to living. But he takes his memories with him. No other person—that is, no other mere man, even among those closest to him—understands all that he remembers and feels: 'The heart knows its own bitterness, and no stranger shares its joy' (*Prov.* 14:10). But there is One who knows—for he is God as well as man—and he is able to sympathize (*Heb.* 4:15). He suffered first, and he remembers. And so the memory-laden Christian, knowing that he has such a friend in Jesus Christ, draws near to the throne of grace time and time again, to 'receive mercy and find grace to help in time of need' (*Heb.* 4:16).

Sometimes people speak of the need to 'let go' of the past, but that is ambiguous language at best—deeply hurtful at worst. True, something is wrong if a person's mourning years later looks no different than it did the day after, still doubled over, still incapable of living. But the language of 'letting go' can communicate something positively false. Imagine the parent who has lost a child being told, 'It's time to let go and move on.' What that sounds like is, 'It's time to stop feeling and start forgetting.' But that parent knows, 'I *can't* forget. And I certainly can't stop feeling.' The Christian's calling is neither to forget nor to remember without emotion, but patiently to rise up, trusting in Christ, and press on. Christ himself was 'a man of sorrows, and acquainted with grief' (*Isa.* 53:3). Thus we who know him honour him when we grieve in a way that fits the hard providences that he himself has appointed for us. And that means grieving with hope in hand—hope which will one day prevail—for he has made us his fellow heirs of a new world.

Of course, these are hard things to contemplate, both the memory of sorrows past as well as the prospect of pains that may yet lie in our future. It is much easier to read and write about these realities than it is to endure them firsthand. Whether past, present or future, trials have a way of testing our heavenly-mindedness. We can almost imagine, like in the book of Job, Satan challenging God about any Christian: 'Yes, I see your servant, how hopeful he looks, how heavenly-minded he seems to be. But let me strike him just one awful blow, and then watch all of his heavenly-mindedness evaporate like the mist it always was. Just watch as he forgets all about heaven—and all about you—and becomes a bitter, backward-facing shell of himself. I've done it before, and I'm sure I can do it again with this one.' How dreadful to contemplate. Has that fearful prospect come true in your own life? Have past sorrows shackled you like so many cold, heavy chains? Christian, child of God, throw them off. Cry out to Christ, 'Set me free!' Run to him with all the sorrows you have ever known. They will not be too much for him to handle. Run to him, and keep running until you meet him in the world to come. Like Bunyan's pilgrim, run and cry, 'Life! life! eternal life!'

What a fascinating feature of human experience is the capacity to remember. Think of it, each of us carrying around in his mind a private library of little films and slideshows that he can replay at any time, some of them sharp and clear, others grainy and worn. And yet what a cruel tyrant memories have become in so many lives. What a hard yoke and a heavy burden weigh on those who are hopeless, living in the past. Like the Apostle Paul, who strained forward and pressed on, let us follow another Master, the one who has gone before us into the future and who bids us join him there. Onward, friends. Onward toward the goal for the prize of the upward call of God in Christ Jesus.

CHAPTER SEVEN

Harps and Clouds

We neglect to set our minds on heaven . . .
Because of a distorted view of what heaven will be like.
So let us clear away the debris of cultural confusion.

YOU can learn a lot about popular assumptions from comic strips. Because the comic strip artist has relatively little space in which to tell his story (usually three or four small panels, and sometimes only one), he regularly relies on readily recognizable images in order to make as much communicative impact as possible.

Now, let's all take a brief image association test. If a comic strip artist wants to sketch a picture his readers will quickly recognize as portraying a heavenly scene, what does he draw? Usually he draws clouds, wings and harps. Perhaps halos are thrown in for good measure.

Whatever the artist's personal beliefs may happen to be, such images reflect popular notions about heaven. And according to those notions, I think we can all agree, heaven will be, frankly, boring. It will be a place of relative inactivity, lacking interest, lacking substance. It will be a cloudy, ethereal place in which folk do little but sit around and play harps (presumably cloudy, ethereal harps). Although the capacity to fly will be a bonus—who has never dreamed of flying?—after a while even the novelty of that mode of transportation will likely wear off. (Just to be clear: no, the

Bible does not teach that we will be able to fly in heaven, but the wings of our comic strips seem to suggest it.)

I must admit, when I picture a world in which we do nothing but sit around and play harps, I am left wondering, 'Who wants that?' And I say that with all due respect to harpists. To my ears the sound of a harp played skilfully, is, well, 'heavenly', and I can only imagine the years of hard work it takes to be able to play one so well. But even the most devoted and enthusiastic of harpists—at least, those who live well-rounded lives—must admit that there has to be more to life than playing the harp. And yet this is the sort of image of heavenly experience that prevails in many minds. One-dimensional. Boring. Static. Disappointing. According to this conception of heaven, the one who arrives there must be left wondering, 'Is this all there is? Is this what I was longing for? Is this what I was promised? Will things pick up after a while? And if so, when?' To the degree that people picture heaven along these lines, we can hardly wonder that they are not drawn to think about it, let alone long for it.

HEAVEN NOW

How might we respond to such notions? Here let us remember the distinction we have already drawn between (1) the intermediate state (that is, heavenly life as it is presently experienced by those who have gone there through death) and (2) the eternal state (that is, life in the new world after the return of Christ).

First, when it comes to the intermediate state, we must readily admit that there is something ethereal about it. Remember, those who are there do not yet possess their resurrection bodies. Plus there is something mysterious about it. What and where is this realm in the created order that we cannot see, and how precisely are its inhabitants passing the time? Plus there is even something temporary about it. Remember, those who are there feel a godly longing for developments yet to take place: 'O Sovereign Lord, holy and true, how long?' is their cry (*Rev.* 6:10). But even conceding all of that, still we must affirm that life for those who are in heaven now is anything but boring. Do you think it boring to know God—Father, Son and Holy Spirit—with an intimacy that makes our knowledge here pale in comparison? 'For now we see in a mirror dimly, but then face to face' (*1 Cor.* 13:12). Do you think it boring to share fellowship with the risen Christ and hail him as King and Redeemer, joining a vast company of those who are doing the same? Do you think it boring to enjoy an unending reunion with believers from ages past, those who lived and died in times so far removed from your own, perhaps those whose books you read or whose hymns you sang or whose example you followed? Do you think it boring to long for the world to come with an intensity that we who remain on earth have never felt? These are realities no comic strip could ever capture, and yet it is precisely these realities that make heaven what it is. The intermediate state may be just that—'intermediate'—but it is certainly not disappointing.

HEAVEN FOREVER

Second, when it comes to the eternal state, we must answer the charge that heaven will be boring with a resounding affirmation of just how exciting and fascinating eternal life will be. In the eternal state we will live rich, full, fulfilling human lives on the solid ground of a new earth, clothed in new bodies, joined in blessed society.

In an effort to grasp this, stop and think about human life as we experience it now. I mean, consider those aspects of human life in which our capacities are engaged and our longings satisfied. Take, for example, an artistic endeavour such as painting. Imagine the deft strokes of the painter, skilfully transferring to the canvas the striking image she has created in her mind, and then imagine her satisfaction—and ours—when she stands back to behold the finished product, a masterpiece of colour and shading, lines and spaces, bold strokes and subtle impressions. The artist takes a proper pride in what she has done, and those who sit in the gallery and study her work for hours on end share in that sense of satisfaction with her. Now, can we imagine that the new world will be one devoid of such artistic expression and achievement? Consider architecture: the way a soaring building lifts our eyes and takes our breath, or the way a well-designed home perfectly and creatively fits the life of the family that lives there. Can we conceive that in the new earth there will be no such creative design and development? Consider athletics. No, not everyone loves sports. But everyone ought to be able to admire the way a skilled athlete employs his well-honed body to scale heights of physical accomplishment. Can we imagine that the new creation will be one in which there is no such running and riding, catching and kicking, diving and jumping, throwing and hitting?

Examples abound. Consider music: the playful improvisation of a jazz trio, or the soaring strains of a symphony orchestra (performing a concerto for harp, perhaps), or the nimble strumming of a guitar virtuoso. Consider science: the curiosity that God's world inspires in us and then the wonder we feel when our curiosity leads us to investigate and discover. Consider travel: the anticipation each of us has felt when setting off to visit some new place, and then the satisfaction of arriving, and then the thrill of taking in some new vista we have never seen before. Consider gardening: the way the gardener thoughtfully plans his plot in his mind, and then slowly, patiently, makes that dream into reality, carefully working the ground, diligently caring for the seeds he has sown, and eventually enjoying the sights and smells that have resulted from his labour. Last (but certainly not least!) consider eating: a thoughtful menu, carefully prepared, making the most of a wide variety of ingredients, beautifully presented, and finally enjoyed, all five senses engaged, with family and friends lovingly gathered around the table.

Of course it is true that each of these aspects of human experience has been marred in some way by humanity's fall into sin and by the divinely imposed curse that resulted. Whether in art or in architecture, whether in science or in travel, we have all seen how sin and frustration distort God's good gifts. Sinful aims are pursued, or sinful strategies are adopted, or brokenness of mind or body leads to failure, or all of the above. But to be marred is not to be destroyed. Even in this world under God's curse man has tasted something of these delights. God made man to make the most of the world he created for him—including man's own created nature—and endowed him with the capacities to do so. In measure, we *have* done so, and we have known something of the satisfaction that results. Just as God looked over the created order as he originally shaped it and took delight in what he had done ('And God saw everything that he had made, and behold, it was very good'—*Gen.* 1:31), man made in God's image has known the experience of using his powers to accomplish and then basking in the outcome. This is human nature. This is human life. Can we imagine that the new world will be one in which none of these activities, none of these delights is known? Remember how wonderful our resurrected bodies will be: imperishable, glorious and powerful (*1 Cor.* 15:42-43). If the new creation is one in which the powers of our new bodies are not used to the uttermost but instead lie dormant, it would seem that God will have left us 'all dressed up with nowhere to go'.

Admittedly the Bible provides no detailed description of what life in the new world will be like. These reflections are somewhat speculative. But this much we can say without hesitation: life in the new world will be more, and not less, than life as we know it now. God's intention is to exalt creation—not to diminish it, not to freeze it, not to replace it with something altogether different. God's design is to glorify human nature, body and soul—not to change it into something unrecognizable. When we stop and think about all of these ways in which we find our nature so wonderfully engaged in the present life (art, architecture, athletics, *etc.*), we should only be thrilled at the thought of what awaits us in the future life. It will be more. It will be better. It will not be boring!

This is why there is nothing silly or sub-Christian about imagining heaven in terms of physical blessings we experience here on earth. For example, I enjoy cycling, and I can say, 'Won't it be wonderful in the new world to find that the climbing of hills is always exhilarating, never dispiriting!' No, I cannot know precisely the sorts of activities that will be available to us in that world, but I can use earthly activities familiar to me now as material for the imagination. There is something biblical, even prophetic, about this. Recall how the Old Testament prophets would picture the world to come by drawing upon the ordinary experience of the people. Read, for example, Isaiah's description of the new creation in Isaiah 65:17-25. Isaiah (indeed, the Lord himself speaking through Isaiah) pointed Israel forward to a world they could only imagine, and in order to make it easier for them to do just that—to imagine—he incorporated into his prophetic portrayal aspects of earthly life they would have known well. Yes, we need to bear in mind that knowing God is the main thing—that is what will make heaven heavenly. Thus we dare not reduce heaven to things like cycling and travelling and eating. But there is nothing wrong—indeed there is something quite fruitful—about imagining just how abundant our life with God in God's new world will be, and making use of the familiar in order to do so.

This also helps allay the suspicion we noted before that being heavenly-minded means being of no earthly good. After all, the truth we are considering here is the truth that heaven (that is, the eternal state) . . . will be *earthly!* New bodies. New earth. New society. Abundant human life. Think of it: if eternal life will fully engage us, mind and body, as we live on glorified solid ground, then meditating upon the glories of that world will give us a renewed— not a diminished—appreciation for mind-and-body, solid-ground life in the present. Such meditations, instead of distracting us from earthly concerns, serve to remind us of the goodness of creation as the home of humankind and of the responsibility we bear to make the most of it accordingly.

FRUSTRATED BY THE BIBLE?

As I noted above, the Bible does not paint for us a detailed picture of what heavenly life will be like. We can imagine that this very fact might become yet another hindrance to heavenly-mindedness. 'When it comes to heaven', someone might say, 'the Bible seems to be a blank slate. How can I possibly set my mind on heaven when the Bible doesn't give me any place to set it. What's the point? Why don't we just put it out of mind until we get there. Heaven is one big question mark right now, and the last thing I need in my life is more frustration!'

The answer to this is two-fold. First, the Bible is not altogether silent about the world above and the world to come. Yes, we do have lingering questions, but in the Bible God has given us some answers too, which we have already traced out. Heaven now is a place of purity, praise, peace and pining. Heaven to come will be a new world populated by God's new humanity, and life there will be rich and full. Now and forevermore, those in heaven have left sin and sorrows behind. So says the Bible about heavenly life.

Second, though it is true that Scripture does not paint for us a detailed heaven landscape (shall we call it a 'heavenscape'?), that should have the effect, not of discouraging or frustrating us, but of thrilling us. Imagine the little boy who has never been to an amusement park, and whose parents have told him that a family vacation to Disney World is just a few months away. Perhaps in the past the boy has ridden a small ride or two at the local city fair. Perhaps he has tasted cotton candy or a funnel cake once or twice before. But never before has he ever gone anywhere quite like the kid heaven that is Disney World. Do you think that will lead him to block it out of his mind? Do you think the boy will conclude, 'Because I can't imagine what a giant amusement park will be like, I'm not going to think about it until we get there'? Not likely! If anything, the sense of uncertainty he feels will only fuel his desire to go there, and thus will have him wondering day and night (perhaps even losing sleep at night) what it will be like to be there. Remember, he has ridden rides and tasted carnival sweets before, so he has enjoyed foretastes of Disney glory. The combination of his past experience with his future longings makes him a positively Disney-obsessed little fellow.

This ought to be the Christian's experience with respect to his heavenly future. What he *does* know and what he does *not* know ought to combine to foster wondering and longing. What he has experienced (love, joy, worship, fellowship, service, satisfaction, even though stained by sin), combined with what he can only imagine (life without sin, life in the presence of God, seeing Christ, joining the saints, a glorious body, a glorious world), creates fascination instead of frustration. He does not block heaven out of his mind. He does not want to do so.

HARPS AND CLOUDS, REVISITED

We began this lesson by observing the popular notions about heaven we see reflected in comic strips. Lest I be misunderstood, I enjoy a good comic strip as much as the next man. In fact, the crafting of such mini-stories with clever words and potent pictures represents yet another one of the ways in which man uses his powers to function as divine image-bearer. So let it be praised. But the persistence of these ridiculous notions about heaven is not so praiseworthy, and to some degree actually reflects man's posture of rebellion against his Creator. Paul teaches us in Romans 1 that the human race is engaged in a desperate and futile campaign to do away with God, trying to 'suppress the truth' about God known to all (verse 18), and this helps to explain why the idea of a boring heaven is so widespread. After all, it is much easier to get heaven and God out of your thinking if heavenly life with God is pictured as so unpalatable, so foreign to human nature. Make heaven out to be ridiculous, and then God seems to be ridiculous too, and then so does Christianity as a whole and all who embrace it, and by then you have armed yourself with apparently good reason to keep disbelieving. No doubt some, if not many, reduce the idea of heaven to something so dull for just this reason, if only subconsciously. Caricature can serve the purpose of evasion and denial. Conversely, how much more difficult it is to do away with God in your thinking when the prospect of eternal life with him resonates within your soul, appealing to your deepest human desires and thrilling you with the vision of those desires unendingly satisfied.

So the next time you see one of those pictures portraying people in heaven, wings on their backs, harps in their hands, go ahead and laugh if the comic strip is funny. Sometimes they are. Enjoy the thoughtful combination of words and images. Marvel at the creativity with which an artist can tell a good story in a small space. And then, finally, go ahead and rejoice at the thought that the life to come—Christian, *your* life to come—will be far more wonderful than you can imagine. No boredom there, you can count on that.

CHAPTER EIGHT

This Vanishing Vapour

We neglect to set our minds on heaven . . .
Because of a failure to come to grips with the fragility of human life.
So let us be reminded that human life is a mist that soon vanishes.

IN his work *Christ-Centered Preaching,* Bryan Chapell offers a
helpful catalogue of types of sermon introductions. You might
introduce your sermon, he notes, with a human-interest account,
or with a simple assertion, or with a provocative question, or with
a startling statement, and then he mentions a few other possibilities.[1] It strikes me that his counsels are valuable for writers as well
as preachers.

So, in the case of this chapter, how might I introduce the awful matter of mortality? How should I broach the serious subject
of your impending dying? It's hard to know just how to begin.
Which type of introduction shall I choose? I might take a cir-
cuitous route—a human-interest account, perhaps, to ease us gently into the subject—but would such an introduction best serve
the purpose? No, my sense is that the simple, startling statement
approach is called for here. Let us dispense with pleasantries. Let
us take the direct route. Here are two such statements:

(1) You might die today. *Today.*

(2) Even if you live a long life, in the grand scheme of things you
will die soon. *Very soon.*

[1] Bryan Chappell, *Christ-Centered Preaching* (Grand Rapids, Michigan: Baker,
1997), pp. 236-38

Here endeth the introduction.

LOW VISIBILITY

Perhaps you yourself do not find those two simple statements terribly startling. Certainly no one in his right mind would dispute them. Even so, is there not something at least a little jarring about them? Those assertions strike us like a splash of ice-cold water in the face. Why is that the case? Is it because the thought of our mortality is so unpleasant? Yes, the explanation lies partly there, but not entirely. The thought of our mortality is not only unpleasant: it is also offensive. It pierces us in our pride. It stings us in our sinfulness. It lays us low. ('What do you mean, I'm not the master of my fate? What do you mean, I'm not as deserving as I'd thought?') And who wants that? So we push it out of mind and, practically speaking, lapse into delusions of immortality. We go on living as if we will always go on living, tomorrow to follow today just as certainly as today followed yesterday, *ad infinitum.* John Calvin observed this:

> If some corpse is being buried, or we walk among graves, because the likeness of death then meets our eyes, we, I confess, philosophize brilliantly concerning the vanity of this life. Yet even this we do not do consistently, for often all these things affect us not one bit. But when it happens, our philosophy is for the moment; it vanishes as soon as we turn our backs, and leaves not a trace of remembrance behind it. In the end, like applause in the theatre for some pleasing spectacle, it evaporates.[2]

It is sometimes claimed that we who live in the twenty-first century find it easier to push death out of mind than did those of previous generations. After all, infant and child mortality rates

[2] Calvin, *Institutes,* vol. 1, p. 714.

are now much lower, and the quality of medical care is now much higher, and so average life expectancy is now much longer, plus hospitals and hospices and nursing homes remove death from view, and then funeral homes dress up death for our view. No doubt there is some truth in this claim, but those words of Calvin—written not in the twenty-first century but in the sixteenth—show us that there is something perennial, something timeless about this phenomenon. Throughout the ages men and women have experienced this, and we still do: we get some glimpse of the end that lies in store for every person, and as a result we find ourselves keenly aware of that sobering reality, but before too long the fog rolls back in and visibility diminishes. The impression of dying fades, and only the expectation of living remains.

In the interest of clarity, let me say that it is perfectly natural that the prospect of death will be more or less at the forefront of our minds depending upon recent events in our lives. We are finite creatures, after all. At different times we find ourselves especially sensible of different realities. This is understandable. But it is not understandable, not acceptable, when issues of death and destiny are effectively pushed to the back of the shelf in an out-of-the-way cabinet in a dimly lit cellar in our minds and left there, dusty and unwelcome and finally forgotten.

Now, what does this have to do with heavenly-mindedness? Well, if our sense of the reality of death evaporates, our sense of the nearness of heaven will evaporate with it. For the Christian death now serves as the great transition point between life here and life above, his passing through that thinner-than-paper-thin curtain between two worlds. For the believer heaven is always just on the other side of that curtain, ever but a moment away (that is, the moment of his death, should Christ not return first). Therefore push death far out of mind, or passively let it drift there like wood left to itself on the water, and the result is that heaven ends up there too—far out of mind. Instead of 'setting our minds on things above', we lose sight of the fact that there is an 'above' in the first place. In short, we set our minds on the one thing that seems real to us, which is life as we know it, here below, day after day.

PUT IN OUR PLACE

What accounts for this phenomenon, this commonly experienced 'evaporation' of the mindfulness of our mortality? How does this come about? It comes about because two truths, in particular, fade from view (or are wilfully, violently shoved from view): the first is our dependence upon God as the moment-by-moment sustainer of our lives; the second is the curse of death which that same God justly imposed upon the human race on account of our fall into sin. Consider these two truths.

1. Our dependence

Perhaps nowhere in all of Scripture do we read of our reliance upon God for survival as clearly as we do in Psalm 104. Having considered creatures of all sorts, humans and animals included, the Psalmist observes, 'These all look to you, to give them their food in due season' (verse 27). Then he adds, 'When you give it to them, they gather it up; when you open your hand, they are filled with good things' (verse 28). In other words, we creatures survive because the Creator sustains. But then the Psalmist acknowledges that the converse is also true: 'When you hide your face, they are dismayed; when you take away their breath, they die and return to their dust' (verse 29). In other words, when the Creator ceases to sustain, we creatures cease to survive. It's as simple as that.

It is worth noting that the Creator sustains his creatures according to the particular creaturely natures with which he has endowed them. For example, he sustains us human beings by preserving us with all of our human needs of mind and body intact (needs for food and shelter, air and water, work and play, family and friends, and so forth), and providentially meeting those needs by his kind and steady superintendence of cause-and-effect in the world. The same Psalm 104 recognizes this: 'You cause the grass to grow for the livestock and plants for man to cultivate, that he may bring forth food from the earth and wine to gladden the heart of man, oil to make his face shine and bread to strengthen man's heart' (verses 14-15). But to recognize the cause-and-effect character of God's sustaining care is not to deny that care, only to analyze it, even celebrate it. By observing these realities (the farmer farms, the grocer sells, the skilful chef skilfully prepares, *etc.*), we have not thereby removed God from the picture, rather we have filled in the picture of God's provision with beautiful biblical colour.

Those familiar with United States history know of the Declaration of Independence of 1776, which both announced and defended the dissolving of political bands with a kingdom across the sea. Well, think of this Psalm 104 passage as a biblical 'Declaration of Dependence'. In the course of human events God upholds us every moment, gives us every breath, provides us every meal. 'In him we live and move and have our being' (*Acts* 17:28). And that is a Creator-creature band that shall never be dissolved.

The Apostle Paul names God as the one 'who alone has immortality' (*1 Tim.* 6:16). That is, God alone is life—it simply cannot be that he would ever cease to be—whereas we creatures only keep living insofar as he is pleased to keep us living. Will all human beings continue existing forever, even beyond this life? Yes. Will all believers continue living joyfully forever in God's new world? Also yes. But all of that follows from God's good pleasure, not from any intrinsic life-sustaining power in ourselves. And if it is his good pleasure, for good and just reasons, that any one of his creatures should cease to enjoy life on earth, then that ceasing follows too. Which brings us to the second point . . .

2. The curse of death

There is a good and just reason why earthly human life comes to an end, and that reason is human sin. 'The wages of sin is death', says Paul (*Rom.* 6:23). More fully, the consequence of Adam's rebellion against the immortal, life-sustaining God was the institution of the curse of death: the human race, cut off from fellowship with God, would find this Creator-creature alienation symbolized in the eventual putting asunder of body and soul upon the body's final breakdown.

Notice, the idea is not that each person's death comes about as the direct consequence of one of the sins he committed in his own lifetime. The curse does not usually work that way (though sometimes it does). Rather, the reality is that the whole human race now suffers this end—Christians and non-Christians alike—and it can be traced back to our rising up against God in Genesis 3. And yes, that was 'our' rising up against God, because Adam represented us—all of us—very well, indeed.

Rightly Humbled

I said before that the thought of our mortality offends us, piercing us in our pride. Reflecting upon the two truths we have just considered helps us to see how that is so. First, we like to think that we are self-sufficient, even self-sustaining, but the Bible puts us in our place by declaring our dependence. We are not self-sustaining, but God-sustained. Second, we like to think that the human race (our foibles and idiosyncrasies and off-days notwithstanding) is basically good, but the Bible declares that we die because we deserve to die for our original rebellion in the Garden with all of its subsequent manifestations. And how many are those manifestations! In short, the very fact that each of us is going to die—maybe today, certainly eventually—testifies to two humbling truths:

(1) We are not so great, and (2) We are not so good. And humbling truths can be unpalatable truths. And unpalatable truths are regularly downplayed, or dismissed, or denied.

'But certainly not among Christians', you say. 'I mean, after all, we're Bible-believers. We believe Romans 6:23 ("the wages of sin is death"). And we believe Hebrews 9:27 ("it is appointed for man to die once, and after that comes judgment"). We're not living in denial. Our eyes are wide open to the Bible, and to hard reality too. Certainly we're immune to this condition you're describing.'

Are we? Really?

Remember, the condition I'm describing boils down to pride: 'I do a pretty good job on my own living and loving others from day to day.' Are we believers immune to that kind of pride, even though we, of all people, should know better?

Have you ever heard a preacher preface a remark with 'I don't know about you, but . . .'? Usually what follows is something like 'I struggle with this sin', or 'I have to deal with that difficulty.' 'I don't know about you, but sometimes I have a hard time trusting God.' Or 'I don't know about you, but sometimes my life feels pretty chaotic.' This is the preacher's homely, self-deprecating, 'aw shucks' way of pointing out some temptation that is common to man. Whenever I hear that preface I cringe, because I find myself thinking, 'Oh, come now, admit it, you know very well about me! Your whole point is that we all struggle with the sin or deal with the difficulty you're spotlighting. You *do* know about me. So straighten up like a man already and say it!' Well then, to be consistent, I'll straighten up and say it here: Reader, I do know about you, and about me too. Pride is a reality in your life, and in mine too. Even if you call yourself a Christian, you are not immune to this. Practical forgetfulness of your dependence and of the curse of death ever crouches at the door. And insofar as you lapse into that forgetfulness, you effectively block out your own mortality. And insofar as you block out your own mortality, you block out heaven too. These mental blocks must be torn down.

SUDDEN DEATH

Remember the first of the two simple statements with which we began: 'you might die today'. I mean that to be taken quite concretely. As you read this, what is the date on the calendar? That, for you, is what I mean by 'today'. That date may be engraved on your tombstone. Picture that. Simple and startling.

Jesus himself told a simple story meant to teach this very lesson:

> The land of a rich man produced plentifully, and he thought to himself, 'What shall I do, for I have nowhere to store my crops?' And he said, 'I will do this: I will tear down my barns and build larger ones, and there I will store all my grain and my goods. And I will say to my soul, Soul, you have ample goods laid up for many years; relax, eat, drink, be merry' (*Luke* 12:16-19).

But then Jesus' parable took a powerful turn: 'God said to him, "Fool! This night your soul is required of you, and the things you have prepared, whose will they be?"' (verse 20). Notice: 'this night'. Not 'next week'. Not even 'tomorrow morning'. 'This night your soul is required of you.' No doubt the rich man *did* have ample goods laid up for many years. His fatal mistake was to assume that he would have those many years too. It is all too easy, and all too common, to make such an assumption. Real life examples are not hard to find. In an interview for *Rolling Stone* magazine, John Lennon once suggested that he might return to touring after a long hiatus in his recording career. 'We're born-again rockers, and we're starting over', he said. 'There's plenty of time, right? Plenty of time.' He said that on December 5, 1980. Three days later he was dead.

The letter written by the Apostle James breathes the spirit of the earthly sayings of Jesus in many passages. Just as Jesus told that story about a rich man who blocked out the possibility of unexpected death, James addressed businessmen who had fallen into the same folly:

> Come now, you who say, 'Today or tomorrow we will go into such and such a town and spend a year there and trade and make a profit'—yet you do not know what tomorrow will bring. What is your life? For you are a mist that appears for a little time and then vanishes. Instead you ought to say, 'If the Lord wills, we will live and do this or that.' As it is, you boast in your arrogance. All such boasting is evil (*James* 4:13-16).

You see, James is not merely teaching them. He is rebuking them. He says more than 'you are a mist'. He says, in effect, 'You have *forgotten* that you are a mist. You're banking on tomorrow, but the fact is, by tomorrow you may no longer be here, trading and making profits like you are today.' They were prone to forget that fact. We are too.

I have found it a helpful practice to remind myself every once in a while of the following reality when I am driving from one place to another: it is more certain I will reach heaven than it is I will reach my destination on this drive. If I happen to be returning to the Fairfax, Virginia house in which I live, I can put it this way: it is more certain I will reach my heavenly home than it is I will reach my earthly one. Not surprisingly, those reflections come more easily to mind if my route home includes the Washington, D.C. Beltway! Does any one of us need to be reminded that death can strike suddenly when we are behind the wheel, since another car can strike suddenly thanks to carelessness, or bad weather, or some other factor?

Notice I said, 'every once in a while'. This is not a reality with which I am morbidly obsessed. I do not grip the steering wheel with white-knuckled anxiety every time I drive, wondering about every oncoming vehicle, 'Is that the one that's going to take me home? Or is it that one? Or is it that one? . . .' But every once in a while I do make a point to bring it to mind. Of course, if one of my children asks me a question from the backseat that elicits from me a brief heavenly observation (see the Introduction), then this reality is immediately brought to mind without any great effort on my part! However it happens, deliberately or accidentally, it is good for us, at least occasionally, to be reminded.

LIFE'S SPAN

The same is true, not only of the potential of unexpected death, but also of the relative brevity of even the longest of earthly lives. Remember the second of the two simple statements with which we began: 'even if you live a long life, in the grand scheme of things you will die soon'.

Listen to Moses: 'The years of our life are seventy, or even by reason of strength eighty; yet their span is but toil and trouble; they are soon gone, and we fly away' (*Psa.* 90:10). Notice, even if we live to reach eighty, those eighty years are 'soon gone'. Remember James' language: 'What is your life? For you are a mist that appears for a little time and then vanishes' (*James* 4:14). That assessment—'a little time'—applies just as much to the man who dies at eighty as to the boy who dies at eighteen. Behind both of their lives stands the backdrop of eternity, and against that backdrop even eighty years—even eight hundred—seems awfully short. A little time. Soon gone.

When our children were babies, strapped snugly into their strollers or resting peacefully against our shoulders as we held them in our arms, friends and strangers alike would say to us, 'Enjoy these years. They'll be gone before you know it.' Most parents of small children hear those words at some point. 'Trust me: blink, and they'll be off to college!' If we can say that about the first eighteen years of parenting, can we not also say it about the whole span of life? 'These years will be gone before you know it.' Yes, we can say that. Moses did. James did. Some wise, elderly folk say it today. Will we listen?

FROM DARKNESS TO LIGHT

I wonder, do I run the risk of seeming morbid by devoting an entire chapter to death, urging you to ponder that it might befall you at any moment, noting that death will 'soon' cut short even long earthly lives? Do I run the risk of emerging as New Hope Presbyterian Church's Associate Pastor for Gloom? Well, I say, let the risk be run. Hopefully there is more than enough gospel light in the pages before and after this to overcome this present chapter's darkness. But the fact remains that the darkness of death is real, and no one can know precisely when that darkness will descend upon him, and everyone ought to know that eventually it will, and sometimes we do need simple, startling statements and powerful parables and arresting images to remind us of these realities.

Christians in ages past who spoke freely and regularly about living in light of dying tend to be dismissed in our enlightened age as gloomy, death-obsessed eccentrics, often labelled with that dirty word 'Puritan'. But I ask you: who are the truly enlightened ones? The Puritan Lewis Bayly, in a diagram introducing his seventeenth-century devotional manual, *The Practice of Piety*, summed up the Christian life as consisting '1. In knowing' biblical truth and '2. In glorifying God aright', then glorifying God he further divided into '1. By thy Life' and '2. By thy Death', and then that last point he further unpacked in terms of dying '1. In the Lord' and '2. For the Lord' (that is, martyrdom).[3] In other words, Bayly put mindfulness of death front-and-centre in his description of Christian faithfulness. And that, among other things, is what makes *The Practice of Piety* (and other works like it) breathe an air of biblical realism. Only in a world gone mad could such an outlook be laughed off as eccentric.

Remember, I am not saying, think about death constantly. I am saying, think about these things as regularly as you need to in order for them to seem real to you. Some Christians, more affected than others by the delusions of immortality that characterise the surrounding culture, may need to bring these things to mind more frequently. And I am also saying, whenever you do think about them, don't forget to keep going and move in your thinking from darkness to light, from death to life, from curse to blessing, from this age to the age to come. True, Romans 6:23 affirms that 'the wages of sin is death', but it affirms more: 'the wages of sin is death, but the free gift of God is eternal life in Christ Jesus our Lord'.

You see, that is where our meditations are meant to arrive. In eternal life. In heaven. In joy. The aim is not to be gloomy, but heavenly, and if I aim to be heavenly then I simply must come to grips with the nearness of my own upcoming earth-to-heaven move. In the blink of an eye I will be with Christ in paradise. Simple. Startling. Wonderful.

[3] Lewis Bayly, *The Practice of Piety: Directing a Christian How to Walk, that He May Please God, Amplified by the Author*, 59th edition, corrected (London: Printed for Daniel Midwinter, at the Three Crowns in St. Paul's Church-Yard, 1734 [First Edition, 1610]), p. 2.

CHAPTER NINE

Get Wisdom

We neglect to set our minds on heaven . . .
Because of a confused understanding of what it means to live by God's will.
So let us heed the Bible's call to live by wisdom.

'WHAT is God's will for my life?'

That is the heartfelt cry of many Christians. Perhaps you yourself have uttered that cry at one point or another. Perhaps you have done so already today, three times before noon!

And it is an understandable cry. After all, did our Saviour not teach us to pray, 'Our Father in heaven . . . your will be done, on earth as it is in heaven'? (*Matt.* 6:9-10). Does the Christian not pray along those lines? Does the Christian not desire to see the will of God realized on earth—indeed, in his own earthly life? Of course he does, and rightly so.

Unfortunately, it is precisely in the matter of knowing and doing God's will that some Christians go wrong. I do not mean that they come to incorrect conclusions about what God's will is. I mean something more fundamental than that: they go wrong about the very idea of what it means to know and obey the will of God in the first place.

The view of the Christian life that some have embraced is what we might label the Circumstance view. The thinking goes something like this. God's will for my life is a set of precise circumstances that he has in mind for me (a particular job to do, a specific house to live in, a particular person to marry, and so forth), and my responsibility is to figure out just what those circumstances are and then to act in such a way as to make them come true. If I succeed at doing so—that is, succeed in divining where God wants me to be and then getting there—then I am living 'in the centre of God's will'. But to the degree that I have not quite landed in those God-appointed circumstances, I am removed from the centre of his will—and I had better get to work trying to figure out where I went wrong and how to get to the centre after all.

And just how is the Christian supposed to do that—that is, figure out what these circumstances are that God intends for him? Here the game really begins. Some Christians go so far as to expect personalized whispers from God—individually directed words of special revelation in which God tells us in no uncertain terms what the details of our lives are supposed to be. 'There I was, driving down the road, when suddenly I heard this voice say, "Ben, it's time to move your family to Boston." I just know it was God.' Other Christians, rightly dubious about such claims of personalized special revelation, still search the past and present details of their lives for clues, interpreting blessings and frustrations as hints from God as to which course of action they ought to pursue. Ben tells you, 'We had our hearts set on buying that house near the university, but when another family put a contract on the house before we did, well, we just knew it was God's will that we move to Boston. We felt his leading.'

Now, what is wrong with this Circumstance view of guidance and the will of God?

For starters, it makes for persistent and paralyzing frustration in the Christian life. On the one hand, those who listen for personalized words from the Lord either do not experience what they are waiting to experience, or, if they do (better: if they *think* they do), they have no solid ground for being sure it actually was a divine word they heard in the first place. 'Come to think of it, maybe it wasn't the Lord who told me to move to Boston. Maybe it was just an idea that crossed my mind. Or maybe I misheard the words of the song that was playing on the car radio. Maybe we should stay. How can I be sure?'

On the other hand, those who try to interpret their past and present circumstances as so many clues for future conduct find themselves wrapped up in a maddening exercise of code-breaking—and constantly plagued by the fear that they may not have successfully broken the code after all. 'On second thought, maybe the fact that we couldn't buy that house near the university was God's signal that we shouldn't move anywhere, or that we should move down the street, or that we should put an addition on our current house. Which is it?' And so back they go to the tea leaves, trying to figure things out, trying to please a Father in heaven who seems to hide from his children what he wants them to do—a Creator who challenges weak, finite creatures to read the Infinite mind.

And even when they finally make a decision they may be forever haunted by the fear they made the wrong one. Years ago they stood at a fork in the road, with two apparently God-honouring options before them, and they asked in prayer, 'Lord, where do you want me to go now? Right or left?' They thought they heard him say—or at least hint—'right', but now they wonder, 'What if I misread the clues? What if I should have gone left? And if so, can I be living in the centre of God's will ever again?'

The heart of the matter is this: the Circumstance view of the Christian life reflects a failure to distinguish between two biblical understandings of God's will, which have been called his 'will of precept' and his 'will of decree'. God's will of precept, on the one hand, is his commandments. Consider, for example, 1 Thessalonians 4:3: 'For this is the will of God, your sanctification: that you abstain from sexual immorality.' God's will of decree, on the other hand, is his eternal plan. Consider Ephesians 1:11: 'In him we have obtained an inheritance, having been predestined according to the purpose of him who works all things according to the counsel of his will.' Put simply:

God's *preceptive* will is what he tells us to do;
God's *decretal* will is what he has determined to bring to pass.

Put another way:

God's *preceptive* will is what we ought to order our lives by;
God's *decretal* will is what he himself certainly orders the world by.

Notice how these two understandings of God's will differ. First, God's will of precept is a matter of principles by which to live, whereas his will of decree covers the circumstances in which we find ourselves. That is, in eternity, before the world began, God decreed what would turn out to be all the circumstances of our lives: both joyful and sorrowful; either temporary or lasting; encompassing those we had a decisive role in bringing about and those we did not; covering work, home, relationships, and every other area of life.

Second, God's will of precept has been revealed for us to read and obey: open up your Bible and you will find in it God's rules for our lives. God's will of decree, however, is known only to him—that is, apart from what has already come to pass and what he has been pleased to reveal in Scripture about the future. This distinction is reflected in Deuteronomy 29:29: 'The secret things belong to the LORD our God, but the things that are revealed belong to us and to our children forever, that we may do all the words of this law.'

Finally, God's precepts, sadly, are often broken: he tells us sinners what to do and we disobey. His decree, however, is never broken, never thwarted, never frustrated: all that God determined in eternity past to bring about, he will most certainly bring about in the unfolding of time. 'Then Job answered the LORD and said: "I know that you can do all things, and that no purpose of yours can be thwarted"' (*Job* 42:1-2).

When it comes to these two understandings of God's will, where does the Circumstance view of the Christian life go wrong? Just here: the will of God that has do with our circumstances, which is his will of decree, is not the will by which we are called to make decisions! We are summoned to live according to his precepts, which are revealed in Scripture, and not according to his decree, which we have no way of knowing ahead of time. In other words, the Christian is right to affirm that God has precise circumstances in mind for him, but he is wrong if he thinks he can learn what they are in advance and then make them happen, and that if he does not make them happen they will never be realized.

In sharp contrast to this Circumstance view is what the Bible actually teaches concerning guidance and God's will. Let's call it the Wisdom view. What is God's will for your life? Good news: you don't have to guess! As I said above, all you have to do is open up your Bible and find there his rules for your life. If you want it boiled down into the form of just one rule, here it is: 'So, whether you eat or drink, or whatever you do, do all to the glory of God' (*1 Cor.* 10:31). If you prefer two, here they are: Jesus said, 'You shall love the Lord your God with all your heart and with all your soul and with all your mind. This is the great and first commandment. And a second is like it: You shall love your neighbour as yourself. On these two commandments depend all the Law and the Prophets' (*Matt.* 22:37-40). If you prefer ten rules, you can find that in the Bible too (*Exod.* 20:1-17). And if you want it stated even more fully than that—well, read the whole Bible. From Genesis to Revelation, in different words and in different ways, God has put in writing his standards for Christian living.

We can imagine the objection: 'But the Bible only provides general principles, and those principles don't tell me what to do in specific situations.' Exactly! And that's where wisdom comes in. Wisdom, according to the Scriptures, is skill in living. Whether it be in the choosing of our words (*Prov.* 25:11) or in the choosing of a spouse (*Prov.* 12:4), in deciding whether to pay a visit to a friend (*Prov.* 25:17) or in diffusing a potentially explosive situation (see Abigail, *1 Sam.* 25), wisdom is know-how. Wisdom entails the capacity to bring the general principles of God's Word to bear upon the specific situations in which we find ourselves. Thus to be wise requires both that we know well the commandments of Scripture and that we understand well the world in which we live, including the 'world' of our own personal lives. Wisdom requires that we pay attention to factors like our own abilities, interests, responsibilities and opportunities, plus the needs of those around us, as we seek to settle on the best course of action in fulfilment of God's imperatives. That takes common sense. That takes using our heads.

So this, after all, is God's will for your life: that you seek sincerely and humbly—thinking, praying, trying, erring, listening to counsel, learning from others' examples, learning from your own mistakes—to obey the commandments of God in the precise circumstances into which his providence has led you. It isn't a matter of trying to guess where he wants you to land down the road and then trying to get there. Rather, the Christian life is a matter of doing your best to apply God's revealed precepts now, including planning wisely for the future. This is God's will. This is what pleases him. This is how to live.

THE HEAVEN CONNECTION

Understandably, you might be wondering at this point if this chapter had accidentally been slipped into the wrong book. Even if you agree with what I have said so far about guidance and God's will, you may be left unclear as to what this has to do with heavenly-mindedness. What's the connection?

Here it is: the Circumstance view of the Christian life diminishes the Christian's sense of the nearness of heaven, because it fosters the suspicion—if not the outright conviction—that death will certainly not come until the Christian reaches the circumstances that God has in mind for him and then lives in those circumstances for some significant period of time.

Take an example. A young Christian man comes to the conclusion, 'It's God's will for my life that I become a lawyer.' (Now, now, don't laugh. The legal profession is an honourable one in the sight of God!) Well, as soon as he concludes that, he cannot help but reason, 'I'm not going to die anytime soon.' He may not actually come out and say that, but now it must be the underlying assumption of his thinking and living. After all, if it is God's will that he become a lawyer, then it must be that he is going to live long enough to study for the LSAT (Law School Admission Test), take the LSAT, do reasonably well on the LSAT—by the way, ask any lawyer: we have already described a process that may take considerable time—and then go to law school, graduate from law school, study for the bar exam, pass the bar exam, and then serve as a lawyer for several years. Otherwise, the will of God will have been thwarted. The practical effect is the pushing of heaven out of the picture, because he cannot conceive that he will be going there for years to come. There is simply too much studying and succeeding and lawyering that has to happen first.

Take another example. That same young man comes to the conclusion, 'It's God's will for my life that I marry Jill.' Well then, it must be that he is going to live long enough to propose to Jill, plan the wedding (or let Jill and her mother plan the wedding), and say 'I do'—and then, presumably, live with Jill for some time in wedded bliss. Of course, if he has never actually introduced himself to Jill, or if he has already proposed marriage to Jill a first time and she said 'No thanks', or if he and Jill are only twelve years old, then this could take a long time, indeed. And as long as it takes, life on earth remains that young man's dominant future horizon. Heaven has receded into the background—far into the background—because all he can see is life on earth, life lived with Jill, because that's God's will, right?

Take a personal example. I set out to write this book not because I had concluded, 'It's God's will for my life that I get a book published on heavenly-mindedness.' Had I allowed myself to think along those lines, then I would have made dying and homecoming into impossibilities, at least for the foreseeable future. I would have slipped into thinking, 'God's certainly going to keep me here long enough to write such a book and then see it through to publication.' And as any author can tell you, that process takes time. Sometimes, it takes a lot of time. How sadly ironic it would have been, had I allowed the writing of a book about heaven to dull my own sense of the nearness of heaven! No, I set out to write this book because I concluded, all things considered (my abilities, my interests, my responsibilities, my opportunities, the prospect of encouraging others, and so forth) that it was a wise course of action. And I set out on that course knowing full well that I do not know what a day may bring (*Prov.* 27:1). I could not know if I would see an earthly tomorrow, let alone ever see this book, written and published, sitting on my shelf. That uncertainty did not make the course of action foolish or leave me dispirited. Quite to the contrary: I dove into this project with zeal and excitement and prayer. But I did so knowing that heaven is ever a breath away, and thus that this particular project might not reach its culmination.

In the same spirit let's revisit the case of the young man we met before. (Given his desire to marry Jill, perhaps we should call him

'Jack'.) It would be right for Jack to set off down the path toward becoming a lawyer, firmly persuaded of the wisdom of doing so, because of his desire to serve the Lord and others in that capacity, plus his aptitude for the consideration of legal matters, plus his freedom from responsibilities that might have made going to law school impractical, plus the available resources (especially time and money) to make it possible. Furthermore, he ought to acknowledge that it was the Lord himself who brought all those things to pass (that is, Jack's desires, skills, freedoms and resources). And yet he ought to take his first step down that path—and every step thereafter—freely admitting the possibility that the next step he takes will be to step into the immediate presence of his Saviour, brought by means of an unexpected death into the blessedness of unrivalled life.

We can say the same thing when it comes to Jack's love for Jill. 'By all means, Jack, if you love her, and if it seems to you that the two of you would make a good fit in marriage, then seek her. And if you ask her and she says "yes", then start planning that wedding (or give steady moral support while Jill and her mother plan the wedding), and do so with excitement and optimism. But never forget that your first love must ever be Jesus Christ, and that he may very well intend for you to join him and his holy ones in heaven long before you and Jill are scheduled to join hands in matrimony. Even when you reach the point of "saving the date" for your wedding ceremony, remember that Jesus Christ has already marked the date of your going to be with him. And he will keep that most blessed reservation.'

It might be objected: 'But if what you're saying is true, where does that leave the idea of "calling"? Can a person not claim, "It's my calling to become a lawyer"? Can there be no such confidence concerning the future?' Let me answer the objection this way: the biblical word 'calling' is a wonderful, ennobling word, but any view of calling that effectively denies that you could die today is an un-biblical view. One's calling amounts to the commandments of God plus the set of circumstances in which those commandments must now be carried out. Thus the lawyer can certainly say, 'It's my call-ing to be a lawyer'... because he is one! (Note, that does not mean he must remain a lawyer—sometimes it is wise to change course—but so long as he is one, that is his calling.) But can the law school student say the same thing, 'It's my calling to be a lawyer'? Well, the student can say, 'It's my calling to be a faithful student', because in God's providence his life is now a student's life. Plus he can say, 'It's my *aim* to be a lawyer', because he has (wisely, we trust) made that his aim for the future, taking into account a host of God-appointed factors. But as soon as he starts thinking, 'It's my calling from God that I turn out to be a lawyer down the road', he has introduced a perilous presumption. Nothing but the passage of time will reveal if his aim is meant to be realized. Who knows what developments may intervene? Remember, Christian, when it comes to calling, God is the caller, not you. And the God who calls is free to call his children into glory whenever he pleases.

The same applies to serving as a minister of the gospel, and oh, how easily the language of 'calling' can be distorted when it comes to entering the ministry. Seminary students of the world, hear me out: if you are in seminary right now, training for pastoral ministry, then your calling (at least right now) is to study for the ministry, because in God's providence, there you are. And your *aim* is to become a minister, because you and others have judged that God has given you the gifts and abilities for that work, so that you have pointed your life and labours in that direction. But you cannot know that you will turn out to be a minister in the future. Only God knows. When I was in seminary, two of our fellow students were struck and killed by a drunk driver. They may have entered seminary, as many of us did, with high hopes of serving God as pastors, and rightly so. And no doubt those two men gave themselves faithfully to their responsibilities as students, because they recognized those responsibilities at the time to be their calling. But then, in an instant, they were called home. Every Christian—no matter his station—must come to grips with the very same possibility. As Moses prayed, 'teach us to number our days that we may get a heart of wisdom' (*Psa.* 90:12).

QUESTION AND ANSWERS

So, Christian, what is God's will for your life? Here are two true answers.

Answer #1: His revealed will, his will of precept, is *certainly* that you love him with all your heart and with all your soul and with all your mind, keeping his commandments, and that you do your best to love him wisely in the circumstances in which he has placed you.

Answer #2: His secret will, his will of decree, *may* be that you make the glorious transition from earth to heaven before this day is done.

Christian, get wisdom.

CHAPTER TEN

Love Your Loved Ones

We neglect to set our minds on heaven . . .
Because of a failure to take steps to prepare others for our departure.
So let us repent of our failure, find forgiveness, and faithfully take
those steps.

L IKE most people, I have attended many funerals over the
years. One funeral that remains fixed in my memory is one
I did not attend. Along with millions of others, I watched it on
television. It was the November 6, 1995 funeral for Yitzhak Rabin,
the Prime Minister of Israel, who had been assassinated in Tel
Aviv just two days before. Of course, the funeral was attended by
dignitaries and heads of state from all over the world, and many of
them gave speeches honouring the slain leader, noting his contributions in the realm of international relations. But the speech that
stuck with me was not delivered by any king or president or prime
minister, but by Rabin's own seventeen-year-old granddaughter,
Noa Ben-Artzi. Here, in English translation, is her eulogy in its
entirety:

> You will forgive me, for I do not want to talk about peace. I
> want to talk about my grandfather. One always wakes up from a
> nightmare. But since yesterday, I have only awakened to a night-
> mare—the nightmare of life without you, and this I cannot bear.
> The television does not stop showing your picture; you are so

alive and tangible that I can almost touch you, but it is only 'almost' because already I cannot.

Grandfather, you were the pillar of fire before the camp and now we are left as only the camp, alone, in the dark, and it is so cold and sad for us. I know we are talking in terms of a national tragedy, but how can you try to comfort an entire people or include it in your personal pain, when grandmother does not stop crying, and we are mute, feeling the enormous void that is left only by your absence.

Few truly knew you. They can still talk a lot about you, but I feel that they know nothing about the depth of the pain, the disaster and, yes, this holocaust, for—at least for us, the family and the friends, who are left only as the camp, without you—our pillar of fire.

Grandfather, you were, and still are, our hero. I want you to know that in all I have ever done, I have always seen you before my eyes. Your esteem and love accompanied us in every step and on every path, and we lived in the light of your values. You never abandoned us, and now they have abandoned you—you, my eternal hero—cold and lonely, and I can do nothing to save you, you who are so wonderful.

People greater than I have already eulogized you, but none of them was fortunate like myself to feel the caress of your warm, soft hands and the warm embrace that was just for us, or your half-smiles which will always say so much, the same smile that is no more, and froze with you. I have no feelings of revenge because my pain and loss are so big, too big. The ground has slipped away from under our feet, and we are trying, somehow, to sit in this empty space that has been left behind, in the meantime, without any particular success. I am incapable of finishing, but it appears that a strange hand, a miserable person, has already finished for me. Having no choice, I part from you, a hero, and ask that you rest in peace, that you think about us and miss us, because we here—down below—love you so much. To the angels of heaven that are accompanying you now, I ask that they watch over you, that they guard you well, because you deserve such a guard. We will love you grandfather, always.[1]

I wonder, was there ever another moment quite like it in the history of television? If so, rarely. It was extraordinary. Imagine the scene. There she stood, this teenage girl, before an assembly of the world's powerful, and she showed them her weakness. Her pain was palpable. Her cry was raw and real. It was as if she said to that august company, 'Speak to me no more of peace processes and lasting legacies. My beloved grandfather is gone. An assassin took him. Death has taken him. And none of you can bring him back.' The other speakers had sought to give Rabin his due as a man and as a statesman. His granddaughter, likewise, sought to honour his memory, although, strangely, by the time she was done she had also given Death its due. By her poignant eulogy she effectively acknowledged the power of the last enemy (*1 Cor.* 15:26), which is the power to remove loved ones from the land of the living while we in our weakness stand by, helpless, watching and weeping. As a Christian listening to her words, I could only add to the revelation of her pain a sense of my own pain for her: a pain borne of the realization that this young woman cried out for her grandfather without the death-conquering hope that only Jesus Christ has to give. It was truly crushing to see.

Why revisit that 1995 moment here in this chapter? My point is this: death remains an enemy, and a powerful one. Friends and family left behind feel its powerful blows. There is the sorrow of great loss, plus there is the potential for profound confusion: 'Why, Lord? Why like this? Why now? What now?' Yes, for the believer

---

[1] Text available at the website of the Israel Ministry of Foreign Affairs: www.mfa.gov.il/MFA.

the sting of death has been removed (*1 Cor.* 15:55-56) since death is now the occasion for his entrance into glory. Yes, Christians confronted with the death of fellow Christians need not 'grieve as others do who have no hope' (*1 Thess.* 4:13). But that does not mean their grief is not real. They still long to see his smile again. Or they still long to feel her caress again. Or they catch glimpses of a smiling face in a photograph, and then that sense of emptiness comes washing over them again in waves. Yes, death remains a powerful enemy.

While we yet live, we have a duty to come to grips with that power, especially with our loved ones in view. Being ready to die means, among other things, taking practical steps now to minimize the sorrow and confusion friends and family will feel when we are taken. Advertisements for life insurance companies sometimes play on our heartstrings by showing us images of weeping widows and children, but is there not a wholesome impact that might be made upon us by those images? Stop and think about what your own death will mean for others, and then you realize: there are things to do now.

What does this have to do with nurturing heavenly-mindedness? The connection is this: knowing you have taken steps to prepare others for your death will strengthen your sense that you are ready to go. Conversely, if whenever I think on heaven my conscience testifies, 'But Paul, you're not ready to go. Just think of all the things you haven't done for your family to minimize the burdens they'll bear when you're gone', then I will likely turn my mind away from that subject as quickly as I can. 'Whoever knows the right thing to do and fails to do it, for him it is sin' (*James* 4:17). We find it uncomfortable to be reminded of our sins of omission, thus we change the subject and seldom come back to it.

If we find this gnawing sense of guilt within our hearts, what is the solution? One word: *Repent.* That means, go to Christ, confess your failures, in that confession seek and receive his forgiveness, and then rise up determined to do by God's grace what you ought to have done all along. Do not live with this guilt which is so spiritually deadening. Instead, deal with it. Take it to Christ, and then go forth in the service of Christ by preparing to die.

THINGS TO DO

The steps we ought to take to prepare for death with our loved ones in mind run the gamut from the mundane to the spiritual. For example, for my wife and me, preparing for death has meant making sure we have adequate life insurance policies in place. We have also made arrangements with another family to take our children into their household should the two of us be taken from life together. With the assistance of an attorney we have had wills prepared in which various financial and medical matters are addressed. Plus I have prepared a set of instructions for my wife covering everything from planning my funeral to knowing where to find the passwords that protect our financial accounts. As mundane as it sounds, I have even sought to keep our family's ever-mounting paperwork filed away in a system she will be able to understand. Should I be suddenly called home, I do not want her to have to crack the code of an inscrutable filing system as she tends to earthly affairs. At that point she will have enough on her mind. Admittedly, I do have a few files labelled 'Stuff', but that way I leave her just a little excitement.

The ever-practical Martin Luther pointed out that attending to such mundane affairs as these helps prevent some of the unpleasantness that commonly follows a person's death. He observed,

> since death marks a farewell from this world and all its activities,
> it is necessary that a man regulate his temporal goods properly
> or as he wishes to have them ordered, lest after his death there

be occasion for squabbles, quarrels, or other misunderstandings among his surviving friends.[2]

No doubt Luther could have told vivid tales of such squabbles he had witnessed. Most likely, around the Luther family dinner table, he told plenty of them!

Of course, there are weightier responsibilities than these—there are *spiritual* responsibilities—that we ought to fulfil to prepare for death. I will mention three of them.

1. First, make it clear to those who love you that as a Christian believer you are at peace with God and ready to go.

We can ill afford to be squeamish about these subjects. Get over the discomfort you may feel when it comes to talking about dying and destiny. That does not mean, talk about these things constantly and with everyone. It does mean, talk about them naturally, and at least occasionally. It could be nothing more than a passing comment you make in a conversation along the way, or it could be a straightforward declaration on your part in the context of an emotional, heart-to-heart discussion with a member of the family. However it comes out, let it come out: let it be known that your faith is in Jesus Christ who died and lives, and not in your own good works, and thus that you are ready to die and eager to be with him. Do not wait, thinking, 'I can talk about these things later, when it's clear my time is coming.' Your time may come in such a way that the opportunity is lost, and these priceless words are never spoken.

As a father, I have made it my goal to set heaven before my children in such a way that, should God take me there today, my wife would be able to say to them, 'Do you remember how Daddy used to talk about heaven? About how wonderful it will be? About

---

[2] Martin Luther, 'A Sermon on Preparing to Die', in *Luther's Works, vol. 42, Devotional Writings I*, ed. Martin O. Dietrich (Philadelphia: Fortress Press, 1969), p. 99.

how excited he was about going there? Well, he's there right now. Yes, we miss him, and so we should cry. But we also love him, and so we should be happy for him. And as we trust in Jesus we can be sure that we'll be with Daddy again. Best of all, we can be sure that we'll be with Jesus too.' And I want my children to be able to answer, 'Yes, Mommy, we remember. Daddy did talk a lot about heaven, didn't he?' The observation has been made that one of the greatest gifts a parent can give his children is the well-founded confidence that he is bound for heaven when death comes. Parents, have you given that gift? Think of all the gifts you *have* given to your children: all the toys you assembled, all the packages you wrapped, all the vacations you provided. Did you give them all those things without ever giving them peace of mind about your standing with God, and thus your eternal destiny? Have you spoken about your faith in Christ and your heavenly hope in such a way as to put to rest any fears they may feel?

2. Second, teach by your words and by your example just how great is the grace of God, for in that way you encourage others that they will be able to carry on without you.

In short, teach your loved ones, 'You don't need me!' Of course, there is a sense in which we do need others: God designed us to flourish in family and community, and we suffer somewhat when those bonds are broken. But even then, his grace is sufficient to sustain us. Show this in your own life. Deal with your own losses and sorrows in such a way as to demonstrate the power of God to console and renew. Then, when the time comes when others have lost you, your legacy will be this: 'I could do all things through him who strengthened me (*Phil.* 4:13) . . . and so can you.' You will have lived that way, and thus will you have charged them to carry on in that same way.

By the way, do you harbour some doubt that God can take care of your loved ones without you? Do you find yourself thinking,

'But they do need me. They couldn't live without me'? If so, then an unbelieving arrogance has crept into your attitude. You are thinking lowly of God, and too highly of yourself. You have effectively removed infinite goodness, unsearchable wisdom and almighty power from God and attributed those things to yourself. Could it be that you have even allowed such arrogance to shape the way you relate to others? For example, some parents treat their children this way. The parents inadvertently magnify their own importance instead of God's—lording it over their children's lives, managing all the details, making all the plans, solving all the problems—thus obscuring the glory of God from view. The result is that the children never grow up into men and women who can live for God and trust in God on their own. Instead they turn out as spiritually stunted Christians who are woefully ill-equipped to deal with the death of their parents—for that matter, to deal with life itself. Of course, a close-knit family is a wonderful thing. But a family that is close in such a way that its members never develop the personal strength to lean on Christ and persevere in the midst of sorrow is close-knit in all the wrong ways.

The same can be said of close-knit churches and the pastors that serve them. All church members, ministers and non-ministers alike, need to learn well the lesson that John Newton taught in this letter, written to a pastor friend about another pastor who had fallen ill:

> I hope that he and you and I shall all so live, as to be missed a little when we are gone. But the Lord standeth not in need of sinful man. And he sometimes takes away his most faithful and honoured ministers in the midst of their usefulness, perhaps [for this reason] among others, that he may show us he can do without them . . . Blessed is the servant whom his Lord when he cometh shall find so doing, with his loins girded up, and his lamp burning.[3]

[3] John Newton, *Wise Counsel: John Newton's Letters to John Ryland, Jr.,* ed. Grant

Yes, blessed is that servant, and blessed also the congregation he serves.

Martin Luther once instructed—actually, we should say 'chided'—his wife Katherine on this very point. Near the end of his life Luther travelled from his home in Wittenberg to the town of Eisleben, and he and his fellow travellers encountered various dangers in the course of the journey. Knowing Katherine to be concerned, he wrote to her from Eisleben,

> you prefer to worry about me instead of letting God worry, as if he were not almighty and could not create ten Doctor Martins, should the old one drown in the Saale, or burn in the oven, or perish in Wolfgang's bird trap.[4] Free me from your worries. I have a caretaker who is better than you and all the angels; . . . he sits at the right hand of God, the almighty Father. Therefore be at peace.[5]

Luther knew that God could easily create ten more just like him should the original be taken away. Our anxiety for others often arises from a diminished view of Christ as every Christian's caretaker and an exaggerated view of ourselves.

May we all take these counsels to heart. Grasp that you are dispensable, and you will better direct others to the One who is not. Though you cannot make the claim, 'I will never leave you nor forsake you', there is a Saviour who can (*Heb.* 13:5). By your testimony lift others' eyes to him, and you will have made a valuable lasting impression for the days when you are gone.

Gordon (Edinburgh: Banner of Truth, 2009), p. 280.

[4] 'drown in the Saale': Luther's travelling party came upon the Saale River overflowing its banks and had to turn back for a time; 'burn in the oven': a fire broke out in the quarters where Luther was staying in Eisleben; 'perish in Wolfgang's bird trap': the editor explains, 'This is a reference to Wolfgang Seberger and his efforts to trap birds in the backyard of the Luther house in Wittenberg.'

[5] Martin Luther, 'To Mrs Martin Luther [Eisleben,] February 7, 1546', in *Luther's Works*, vol. 50, Letters III, ed. and tr. Gottfried G. Krodel (Philadelphia: Fortress Press, 1975), p. 302.

3. Third and final, let the consideration of your own death and its impact on others be an incentive to holy living.

Paul urged Titus to set a godly example in his life and ministry 'so that an opponent may be put to shame, having nothing evil to say about us' (*Titus* 2:7-8). Every Christian should have a similar regard for his own reputation, living as one above reproach, giving no solid ground for others to speak ill of him, and that applies to the things that might be spoken about us after we die. In other words, live now in such a way that there will be no damaging, disheartening revelations about your character and conduct after you are gone. Remember, it is your family and friends—not you—who would have to bear the brunt of those revelations. That includes dealing honourably now with the sins of your past. 'Bear fruits in keeping with repentance' (*Luke* 3:8). Is there someone to whom you owe restitution? Pay it. Is there someone from whom you need to ask forgiveness? Go and confess your sin and ask for it. Is there someone who once wronged you who has sought your forgiveness? Grant it. In short, do whatever needs to be done to make things right. Leave no outstanding spiritual debts on the books.

Perhaps the best way to summarize these various duties is this: 'So whatever you wish that others would do to you, do also to them' (*Matt.* 7:12). Put yourself in the place of the one who is grieving. Have we all not been in that place at some point? Perhaps you are there right now. What do you wish the one who is gone had done while he yet lived? Perhaps he did those things, leaving you grateful even in your tears. Perhaps he did not, leaving you with sorrow upon sorrow. Heed this call: sow now the seeds that will produce a harvest of gratitude when your body lies in the ground. Then will your loved ones lift their eyes and bless your name, and bless the name of the God you loved. Imagine a funeral like that.

CHAPTER ELEVEN

If It's Sunday, It Must Be Heaven

We neglect to set our minds on heaven . . .
Because of a diminished appreciation of the significance of the church's meetings for worship.
So let us grasp again the heavenly character of the church's Sabbath assembly.

B E honest: did you read the dedication page of this book, or did you blow right past it? If you blew past it, here's what you missed: 'To the saints of New Hope Presbyterian Church in Fairfax, Virginia, with whom I share the privilege of going to heaven every Sunday morning at 9:30.' Now, when we meet for worship our congregation is not caught up into the heavenly realms by being transported there physically, nor do we receive special visions of heaven (like Isaiah did, or John) beyond the visions that the Bible itself provides. No, we go to heaven every Sunday morning without leaving the ground, and (hopefully) without going beyond what is written (*1 Cor.* 4:6) in our singing, preaching and praying. In fact, we go to heaven together while remaining in what some might consider a most unlikely setting for such an experience: a fire station meeting hall.

By now you may have guessed my meaning: we the people of New Hope Presbyterian Church (along with the people of every other Christian congregation throughout the world and throughout the ages) go to heaven when we worship in the sense that we enjoy a foretaste of heavenly experience. Corporate worship is heavenly. By 'heavenly' I do not mean 'exquisite' or 'delightful', the way we might describe a delectable dessert as 'heavenly'. (Ironically, a diner at the next table describes the same dessert as 'sinfully delicious'.) No, I mean that the church's worship on earth partakes of heavenly realities. Every part our worship is infused with light from above. Of course, this makes it profoundly 'delightful' after all! Let us consider how this is so.

HEAVEN ON SUNDAY

First, when we meet for worship the *gathering* is heavenly. In Hebrews 12 the writer paints this picture of the world above:

> But you have come to Mount Zion and to the city of the living God, the heavenly Jerusalem, and to innumerable angels in festal gathering, and to the assembly of the firstborn who are enrolled in heaven, and to God, the judge of all, and to the spirits of the righteous made perfect, and to Jesus, the mediator of a new covenant, and to the sprinkled blood that speaks a better word than the blood of Abel (verses 22-24).

Notice that the writer intends his readers to take that description personally: he tells them, 'you have come' to this world. In other words, by coming to Christ they had come to belong to his heavenly kingdom. The same is true of us. That world is now our world. We have joined the ranks of the citizens of heaven ('our citizenship is in heaven'—*Phil.* 3:20). Further, see that we have come to the 'gathering' of angels and the 'assembly' of the redeemed in heaven. In other words, we have come not just to a place or to a people but to an occasion—the glorious occasion of the gathering of that people in that place to meet with God. The Greek word translated 'assembly' in this passage (*ekklesia*) is the same word often translated 'church', for 'assembly' is at the heart of what the church is and does. All this lends heavenly significance to our meetings on the Lord's Day: when we gather for worship on earth, our assemblies are outposts of the church above.

Second, the *singing* is heavenly. As we have already seen, the book of Revelation lets us listen in on songs now sung on high. As we do so, we discover that the themes of their songs run through our songs too. For example, the inhabitants of heaven sing in praise of Christ as Redeemer (*Rev.* 5:9-12). So do we. They sing in the spirit of Moses, praising God as holy and fearful, and blessing him for his great and amazing deeds (*Rev.* 15:3-4). So do we. No, these are not the only songs we sing. We also sing songs (unlike those in heaven) by which we confess our failings and lament our sorrows. But we also lift up words of heavenly praise and joy. For that matter, even in our songs of confession and lamentation we rightly look forward to the day when we will sin and weep no more. The same is true of our praying. Our words spoken, as well as sung, give voice to heavenly sentiments.

Third, the *preaching* is heavenly. By that I mean, not that there will be preaching in heaven, but that faithful preaching resounds with heavenly realities. Jesus Christ is there in heaven, a faithful Redeemer, so in our preaching we proclaim him. The Triune God, Father, Son and Holy Spirit, is intimately known and praised there, so in our sermons we exalt him. Believers who have arrived there enjoy 'rest from their labours' (*Rev.* 14:13), so in our preaching we comfort Christians with the thought that the same rest awaits them. The holy ones who inhabit heaven are just that—*holy ones*—so in our sermons we summon believers to pursue holiness, and encourage them with the promise that their pursuits will not have been in vain. In short, faithful preaching draws back the curtain and reveals heaven. The sight of it is meant to spur us on as we make our way.

Fourth, the *feasting* is heavenly. When Jesus instituted the sacrament of the Lord's Supper, he took a cup and gave it to his disciples, saying, 'I tell you I will not drink again of this fruit of the vine until that day when I drink it new with you in my Father's kingdom' (*Matt.* 26:29). In that moment Jesus pointed them forward to the Messianic banquet to be served in the new creation, and whenever we celebrate the Supper today he does the same for us. He points us forward. Jesus said, 'many will come from east and west and recline at table with Abraham, Isaac, and Jacob in the kingdom of heaven' (*Matt.* 8:11), and no privilege can compare: 'Blessed are those who are invited to the marriage supper of the Lamb' (*Rev.* 19:9). The Lord's Supper is—quite literally—a *foretaste* of that most glorious feast. Though we can hardly imagine it, one day we will share table fellowship with our Saviour in person, and he has given us this sacrament in the meantime both to satisfy our appetite for communion with him now, as well as to whet our appetite for the full communion to come.

Fifth, the *giving* is heavenly. When we place our monetary gifts in the offering plate as a part of corporate worship, this is no mere financial transaction. In this way we honour the Lord and provide for the work of the gospel. We also follow the lead of those who have gone before us into heaven. Consider the example of those who are described in Revelation as 'casting their crowns' before the throne of God in heaven and giving him praise (4:10-11). They have been blessed, even honoured, by God, and yet they worship him by returning to him that which represents their blessedness. Is he not worthy of this? Absolutely. In heaven they declare that the Lamb is worthy to receive our 'wealth' (*Rev.* 5:12). When we give, we add our earthly 'Amen'. We testify, 'Yes, he is worthy. He owns us and all that we have. So let us cast before him a portion of the wealth he has given us, and ask him to do with it what he will.'

Sixth, the *remembering* is heavenly. By that I mean, when we come to worship God we come mindful of, and grateful for, the goodness of God shown us in the past, especially the once-for-all death and resurrection of Jesus Christ, but also God's works in our lives during the week since we last assembled. Here God himself set the pattern: in Genesis 1 we see God ordering and filling creation for six days and then resting on the seventh. That is, in God's own activity there was the combination of working and taking satisfaction in a job (very) well done. In this respect, man made in God's image follows the divine lead: the Sabbath day becomes an opportunity for us to look back upon God's works and acknowledge him for them, including the works he granted us to accomplish as creatures. Will we not do the same in the eternal Sabbath of the new world? Though we cannot know now precisely what we will remember in the world to come about life in this one, and how memory will function in that world, we can know that we will remember. Listen to this heavenly 'remembrance song' sung to Christ: 'Worthy are you to take the scroll and to open its seals, for you were slain, and by your blood you ransomed people for God from every tribe and language and people and nation, and you have made them a kingdom and priests to our God, and they shall reign on the earth' (*Rev.* 5:9-10). You see? In heaven there is, and shall ever be, the memory of Christ's work both for us and in us: his redeeming us from what we were and his transforming us into what we never otherwise would have become. In heaven there will be an eternal celebration, with new understanding, of what God was up to all along in his ordering of human history, including every human life—including yours and mine. And since heavenly life will not end, neither will the experience of God's goodness: he will forever fill us and thrill us in new ways, thus giving us new blessings to remember, thus giving us new stories to tell and new verses to sing. Every Sunday in this life we can look forward to such heavenly remembering . . . and practice it.

IMPLICATIONS

There are several implications of what we have seen so far. Here we move from what is true of worship by definition to what ought to be true of us and the churches to which we belong. Let me set before you four worship-related challenges.

1. Time to Wake Up

'God loves a cheerful giver' (*2 Cor. 9:7*). He also loves a cheerful assembler, and singer, and pray-er, and sermon-hearer, and Supper-partaker, and remember-er. In short, God loves a cheerful worshipper. 'Cheerful' here does not mean sunny and smiley. It means gladly willing, as opposed to sullen and grudging. In such cheerfulness the Lord delights.

Sometimes when we first wake up in the morning, our minds still foggy, there is that split second as we lie in bed when we struggle to remember what day it is. (The older we get, the longer that 'split second' may become.) Then it hits us: 'Oh, that's right, it's Tuesday. And since it's Tuesday that means I have this meeting to attend, or that party to go to, or this errand to run, or that medical appointment to keep.' Depending upon what we have in store that day—whether opportunities that excite us or responsibilities that fill us with dread—our hearts either rise or sink in that moment of realization. We may even find that our bodies rise or sink too: either we dart out of bed, eager to face the day, or we reach over and hit the 'snooze' button on the alarm clock and slink back under the covers in a desperate attempt to stave off the inevitable. 'Please, just another nine minutes. Maybe when I wake up again, Tuesday will magically have become Wednesday. I don't ask for Rip Van Winkle's twenty years. Just twenty-four hours will do.' And then nine minutes later the same pitiful drama is played out again. From one day to the next, our feelings in those first dawning moments may vary considerably. Excitement or dread. Rising up or sinking down. 'Lemme at 'em' or 'Lemme go back to sleep.'

Now here's the question: when that happens to you on Sunday—when after that split second first thing in the morning it hits you, 'Oh, that's right, it's worship day'—be honest: does your heart rise or sink? Do you find yourself gladly willing, or sullen and grudging? There may be no more telling moment the whole day—come to think of it, the whole *week*—than that initial, unguarded moment when your mind suddenly remembers and your heart instantly responds before you have a chance to compose yourself.

I ask you: does that telling Sunday morning moment reveal you to be a reluctant worshipper? If so, then there is a jarring discrepancy between what is true of corporate worship (heavenly glory) and what is true of you, the worshipper (dispiriting disappointment). Do you think the angels and redeemed humans above wish they could hit a 'snooze' button and put off worship for just another nine minutes? Whatever the precise causes may be in your own life, you have managed to lose sight of the heavenly character of corporate worship, and thus of the inestimable privilege it is to participate in it each week. Do not settle for this. Seek to recover (or gain for the first time) a sense of the heavenly in public worship. Make this a matter of meditation and prayer. (And not just on Sundays, by the way. Think and pray about this Monday through Saturday too. Do not wait for the Sabbath day to ready yourself for the Sabbath day.) Look to the Lord for grace to grasp this. Learn to see the church's Sunday services in their true light, which is light from above. Then will you learn to say with the Psalmist, 'I was glad when they said to me, "Let us go to the house of the LORD!"' (*Psa.* 122:1).

And as you seek this, take to heart this word of encouragement: the same God who loves a cheerful worshipper is himself a cheerful Redeemer. That is, he sent his Son to save—and the Son himself came to save—not sullen and grudging, but gladly willing, though fully knowing what it would cost. Through the prophet Jeremiah, the Lord promised to rescue his people from exile and restore them to their land, and to do so with his heart in it: 'I will rejoice in doing them good, and I will plant them in this land in faithfulness, with all my heart and all my soul' (*Jer.* 32:41). Then when the Son came into the world to save, he came in the same willing spirit: 'I delight to do your will, O my God; your law is within my heart' (*Psa.* 40:8; *Heb.* 10:5-7). Thus did Christ show himself to be a true Son, bearing the image of his Father and driven by his Father's own heartfelt concerns. As it was then, so it is now, and so it shall ever be. Our God remains gladly willing to receive our worship, and to give us eyes to see just how wonderful worship is. Our Father in heaven is for us, and not against us. In Christ he has accepted us, and no longer condemns us. Christ himself is a sympathetic heavenly high priest who will never spurn us. The Spirit is the nearest and dearest of friends at work within us. And it is this gracious Triune God we meet with when we assemble. The inhabitants of heaven know this, and they worship accordingly. From our very first waking moment on Sunday morning, let us show ourselves in heart and manner to be their fellow citizens, for that is what we are!

2. How's Your Posture?

In this chapter we have already touched on a number of things that go on during the worship service. Here let us train our attention on the sermon. Consider your experience as a regular sermon-hearer. Let me ask you, what is your posture during the sermon? No, I do not mean your physical posture. As a preacher myself, I look out at the congregation each week from my slightly raised location and see people sitting in a variety of physical positions, and that is perfectly understandable. Some sit back. Some lean forward. Some sit back for a while and then lean forward for a while and then lean back again. Some churches have pews. Some churches have folding chairs. Some churches have non-folding chairs. Some Christians have bad backs, and they can only sit down for so long. Some Christians have young children, and their young children end up on their parents' laps. (Come to think of it, some Christians have young children and bad backs. Perhaps there's a connection.) There are plenty of ways to sit in worship. *Vive la différence!*

But I mean to inquire about your spiritual posture. How is your heart 'positioned' during the sermon? Spiritually, you ought to be sitting on the edge of your seat! Why? Because during the sermon the faithful preacher is drawing back the curtain that separates earth from heaven to give you a glimpse of the world above. Would you sit back, slouched and disinterested and stealing frequent glances at your wristwatch, during such a moment as that? May it never be! And parents, take note: make that your posture during preaching—a spiritual slouch—and your children will very likely learn to 'sit' that way too, just like you. And so your whole family will leave worship each Sunday having shrugged your shoulders at heaven, and then for the next six days you will proceed to live like it, until the next Sunday when you return and do it all over again. No, this is no way to listen. Instead, 'listen up'. Spiritually, sit on the edge of your seat. Sit up, head held high, for the sermon is yet another opportunity to lift your eyes to the world above. And what an extraordinary opportunity that is!

3. Time to Eat

I understand that Christians hold different opinions concerning the question, how frequently should the Lord's Supper be served? In some churches it is served weekly; in others, monthly; in still others, quarterly. In some traditions the administration of the Supper has been an annual affair. Allow me to put my cards on the table: I believe the Lord's Supper, ideally, will be celebrated at least weekly. The Lord himself, by the example of his apostles, and knowing our needs, appointed that the church ought to assemble weekly (that is, on the first day of the week) for corporate worship, and the Lord's Supper is rightly regarded as one of the elements of Christian worship. When we consider the many benefits the Supper provides, it seems strange to conclude that we do not need it just as frequently as we need to gather with God's people in the first place.

One of those many benefits is the reminder the Supper provides, whenever it is administered, of the church's heavenly future. Remember the words of our Saviour: 'I tell you I will not drink again of this fruit of the vine until that day when I drink it new with you in my Father's kingdom' (*Matt.* 26:29). Notice: 'until that day'. The implication is, that day is coming, the day when the marriage supper of the Lamb will be served, and bride (church) and groom (Christ) will feast together. Remember, too, the words of the Apostle Paul: 'For as often as you eat this bread and drink the cup, you proclaim the Lord's death until he comes' (*1 Cor.* 11:26). Notice: 'until he comes'. The implication is, he will come. He will come back and create his new world, and there we will feast with him.

It strikes me as one of the sad ironies of church life today that, in a day in which the church seems relatively weak with respect to heavenly-mindedness, most congregations choose not to celebrate the Lord's Supper each Sunday. The Lord himself has placed into the hands of a weak church a ceremony that with his blessing makes for spiritual strength, including hopefulness for heaven. Why would we refrain from availing ourselves of it as frequently as the Bible's one-day-in-seven? Obviously, a sudden increase in the frequency of communion in churches around the world would not guarantee an accompanying revival of heavenly-mindedness. There are other factors. The wine in the Supper is no magic potion. But when our King has given us a sacrament that has the effect of lifting our eyes to his coming kingdom, why not take him up on it?

Some answer, 'Because if we serve the Supper weekly it will cease to be special. It will become just another tired ceremony. People will go through the motions.' But do you not sing weekly in worship? (Note, 'weekly'. Hopefully not 'weakly'!) Do you not have preaching weekly in worship? Those aspects of the service are just as liable, if not more so, to spiritual tuning out. Should the church sing monthly, or hear preaching quarterly, to make sure people see them as special? No, we expect singing and sermons every Sunday because we know they are so spiritually important—far too important to be put off for an extra week, or two, or twelve. In this respect the Supper is no different.

Of course, it is true that some go through the motions of the Lord's Supper, eating and drinking without understanding and thinking and praying. But let us not be so naïve as to think that that does not happen in churches where communion is served less frequently. In any case, the solution to that problem is not to hold the Supper back from needy Christians, but to provide appropriate pastoral care alongside it (especially teaching and prayer) to help them participate rightly after all, minds informed and hearts engaged. The goal of our ministry ought to be that God's people understand just how needy they are, and how it is that the Lord meets their needs with (among other means) the Supper he has commanded to be observed in his remembrance. Put another way, our goal ought to be that Christ's people so long for his Supper that they would hate to see a Sunday come and go without it.

Therefore let us not delay the feast. We need it too much for that. We need to have our eyes regularly raised to contemplate the banquet that the church's Bridegroom will spread for her when the Eternal Day finally dawns. The Supper meets that need most uniquely.

4. *Watch Your Language*

Let me also challenge you to stop and think about the language you use to refer to the church's weekly meeting. Consider this question: do you tend to use the language of 'going to church' or 'going to worship'? More precisely: do you *ever* use the language of 'going to worship'? And if not, why not?

There is nothing wrong, strictly speaking, with the phrase, 'going to church'. After all, those words accurately describe our signature Sunday activity: we gather with the *church* (that is, the people of God), and we have to *go* (that is, we have to leave home for some gathering place) in order to do so. Still, though this language may be accurate, it does not seem to pack much of a punch anymore. My sense is that in our culture the language of 'going to church' brings to mind for many people little more than going to a particular building in the community in order to attend the (sometimes) inspirational meeting that takes place in that building. In other words, 'churchgoing' brings to mind something largely earth-bound, a form of human behaviour that can be quantified and dissected by pollsters and sociologists (with all due respect to pollsters and sociologists), something belonging to the same category as consumer habits and political party identification. No, it does not have those connotations for all, but it does for many. Far more potent (though far less common) in our context is the language of 'going to worship'. Why? Because that language more clearly captures the exalted character of what the church gathers on Sundays to do, which is the heavenly activity of 'proclaiming the excellencies of him who called you out of darkness into his marvellous light' (*1 Pet.* 2:9). In short, the language of 'worship' tends to lift our eyes. It promotes a rightly lofty conception of the purpose of our Sabbath assembly.

So begin to season your speech, at least on occasion, with the language of 'going to worship'. And if those words sound funny to you as they come out of your mouth, then practice putting it that way. Language matters. Some words simply have a more heavenly ring.

REDEEM YOUR MINUTES

Several years ago a book was published entitled *90 Minutes in Heaven: A True Story of Death and Life,* in which the author claimed to have died in an automobile accident and gone to heaven, spending ninety minutes there experiencing its glories before returning to earthly life. The merits of the book aside, the title makes me smile.[1] I mentioned before that our worship services at New Hope Presbyterian Church start at 9:30. Guess when they end. That's right: 11:00. One hour and a half. Ninety minutes. So when I hear about a book entitled *90 Minutes in Heaven,* I think to myself, 'Big deal. I get that every Sunday. Ninety-three if the sermon runs long!'

Christian, do you find that your own sense of the reality of heaven has run low? If so, then a good step in the direction of recovery is to make the most of something you already do every week, something so familiar you may barely notice it anymore: going to worship on Sunday. Open your eyes and see heaven in that familiar Sunday service, and then you will begin to notice it like never before. Not only so, but you will also begin to take heaven with you (its songs, its prayers, its gospel, its holiness, its Saviour, its God) into Monday through Saturday too, with new devotion.

No excuses, now. Do not plead that the piano in your church is out of tune, or that the choice of songs is not always to your liking, or that the pastor tends to ramble, or that the room is full of

---

[1] Briefly: yes, I read it (call it curiosity; call it research), and no, I would not recommend it. The reader has no reason to believe that the author's vivid dreamlike experience was anything more than purely internal (that is, just like an ordinary dream). To say the least, this should have caused the author to rethink his interpretation of his experience, as well as his decision to put it into writing.

sinners. Remember, the church's worship on earth is a *foretaste*, not the *full taste*. Do not harbour unfair and unrealistic expectations. Heaven is there. You just have to learn to see it and make the most of it. So will you open your eyes and learn to see it? Anyone can see the dross. That takes no spiritual acumen. That serves as no sign of Christian maturity. Blessed is the man who has learned to see the gold. Blessed is the man whose eyes behold heaven. Christian, you have come to the assembly. Do you behold it? May it be so.

CHAPTER TWELVE

The Whole Counsel of God

We neglect to set our minds on heaven . . .
Because of a reluctance to face the Bible's teaching about hell.
So let us overcome that reluctance and believe all that God has
spoken.

'I did not shrink from declaring to you anything that was profitable . . . I did not shrink from declaring to you the whole counsel of God' (*Acts* 20:20, 27).

So said the Apostle Paul to the elders of the church at Ephesus. In Acts 20 he bade them farewell, meeting with them for the last time before heading to his arrest in Jerusalem. Reflecting upon the time of his ministry in Ephesus, Paul testified that he had not held anything back. He had been faithful to declare the wide range of revealed truth entrusted to him, including truths that some may not have wanted to hear. Like the Lord who powerfully converted and commissioned him on the road to Damascus, Paul had hard truths to proclaim as well as hopeful ones—truths about human sin and divine wrath and the necessity of repentance and the certainty of judgment. And proclaim them he did. This was characteristic of his ministry not just in Ephesus, but wherever he went; not just in his preaching, but also in his writing; not just to Jews, but also to Gentiles; not just to the poor, but also to the powerful; and not just in times of freedom, but also when he bore chains.

For example, while in Roman custody he set the hard truths of the gospel before Governor Felix (Paul 'reasoned about righteousness and self-control and the coming judgment') to the point that Felix finally became so alarmed that he sent Paul away (*Acts* 24:25). From start to finish as an apostle of Christ, Paul held nothing back. Otherwise he would have been something less than the faithful 'preacher and apostle and teacher' that Christ had appointed him to be (*2 Tim.* 1:11). Note this, too, about Paul's farewell address in Acts 20: he testified that during his time in Ephesus he 'did not cease night or day to admonish everyone with tears' (*Acts* 20:31). You see, Paul declared the whole counsel of God 'with tears'. He knew the eternal urgency of the moment. He knew the dire needs of his hearers. And it moved him. He spoke fearlessly as one who felt deeply.

How apt and vivid is the language Paul uses there of 'shrinking' from hard truths. Is that not the very temptation the preacher faces, to shrink back, cowering and cowardly, when the time comes to say something unpalatable and unpopular? You can almost picture the preacher, can't you?—drawing back, taking cover, perhaps hiding behind the pulpit, keeping quiet until the moment passes, and then weeping bitterly, Peter-like, at the realization of his own cowardice. Instead of shrinking back, he should have stood firm, and he knows it. Faithful is the minister who follows in Paul's steps instead, declaring the whole counsel of God and doing so with deep affection.

Is there not a lesson here for all of Jesus' disciples? Though not all are called to be preachers, all Christians are called to be thoroughgoing believers—that is, to embrace all that God has revealed in his Word and live accordingly. As the *Westminster Confession of Faith* puts it, this is what genuine faith amounts to:

> By this faith, a Christian believeth to be true whatsoever is revealed in the Word, for the authority of God himself speaking

therein; and acteth differently upon that which each particular passage thereof contains; yielding obedience to the commands, trembling at the threatenings, and embracing the promises of God for this life, and that which is to come (*WCF* 14.2).

Unfortunately, when it comes to the hard truths of Scripture, Christians face a similar temptation to shrink back. When we come face-to-face with some unpleasant aspect of God's revelation, we may find it easiest to keep turning the pages and not turn back, like the police officer who seeks to steer onlookers away from the site of an accident: 'Please keep moving. There's nothing to see here.' Avert your eyes, lest you see something troubling. Keep things upbeat, lest you find yourself unsettled. That's the way to get a good night's sleep. And don't we all want a good night's sleep?

'OK', you say, 'I'll grant it. We face the temptation to turn away from hard truths because we find them unsettling. But what does that have to do with being heavenly-minded? After all, the Bible's teaching about heaven isn't hard; it's light! It isn't unsettling; it's uplifting. It isn't mournful; it's joyful. No one in his right mind would shrink back from something like that.' True, but the Bible's teaching about hell is hard, and there is an inextricable relationship between the doctrine of heaven and the doctrine of hell. To set our minds on heaven (that is, to do so biblically) is to be reminded, at least implicitly, that there is a second eternal destiny so very different from the first. And for some Christians that reminder may be so discomfiting, so painful, that they prefer to push both ideas out of mind altogether. In other words, they end up shrinking back from both truths—the one which ought to make them tremble, and the other which ought to make them rejoice.

But we cannot give up on heaven out of a refusal to come to grips with other doctrines that surround it. Such refusal is simply not an option. If discomfort with the doctrine of hell is getting in the way of your rejoicing in the reality of heaven, then we need to address that discomfort. Let us do so here by noting the Bible's basic teaching on this topic, aiming to arrive at a sound and sober understanding.

REAL

The first truth to be affirmed about hell is that hell is *real*. In this the Bible is unmistakable: the wrath of God is real—'The Lord is a jealous and avenging God; the Lord is avenging and wrathful; the Lord takes vengeance on his adversaries and keeps wrath for his enemies' (*Nah.* 1:2)—and the Bible speaks of a place where nothing but his wrath will be known for all eternity. Jesus warned, 'Do not fear those who kill the body but cannot kill the soul. Rather fear him who can destroy both soul and body in hell' (*Matt.* 10:28). He spoke often of a place of 'outer darkness' where there will be 'weeping and gnashing of teeth' (*Matt.* 8:12).

We should not be misled by the fact that the Bible sometimes uses metaphorical language when it speaks about hell, language that has a figurative ring. This does not mean that hell is not real. As we shall see, the miseries of that place are described in Scripture using a wide variety of dreadful images, and it is not always clear if this or that detail (darkness, for example, or fire) belongs to the metaphor or to the reality. But the figurative character of the language by no means diminishes the awfulness of the reality. To the contrary, the proper impact of the Bible's manifold, nightmarish portrayal is to make us shudder.

Here we can assert about hell some of the same things we asserted previously about heaven. In particular, hell must be a time-and-space realm within the created order. It must be some sort of 'there'—a location, a destination—where creatures can go, though its precise relationship to our realm is left mysterious to us now. To clear away one misconception, hell is not a place where God is absent, where human beings are separated from God altogether.

Remember, there is no square inch in all creation where God is not fully present. Instead, hell is the realm where God is fully present manifesting wrath instead of grace. Thus, as it has been rightly observed, those who are there wish that God were absent, and their pain, in part, comes from the knowledge that that will never be.

You see, hell is the destiny of those who die unrepentant and unforgiven. In this life many never return to God confessing their rebellion against his rule. They never come to Jesus Christ in whom alone forgiveness is to be found. In short, they never surrender, laying down their arms and accepting God's gracious terms of peace. Therefore in death they go to meet God unprotected from his just wrath. It is worth emphasizing that hell is the destiny every human being deserves, for we are all by nature sons and daughters of Adam—represented by him when he first sinned and now rebels ourselves, adding our own sins day after day. 'All have sinned and fall short of the glory of God' (*Rom.* 3:23). Put most strongly, we are all by nature 'haters of God' (*Rom.* 1:30). And the God we have hated, the God against whom we have sinned, is a God of infinite holiness. Thus we are all 'by nature children of wrath' (*Eph.* 2:3). We all deserve the outpouring of divine anger. The difference between the believer and the unbeliever is not intrinsic deserving, but divine forgiveness. The believer is forgiven thanks to the cross, and thus spared; the unbeliever is neither. Because the unbeliever has not availed himself of the blood of the Passover Lamb (which is Christ, *1 Cor.* 5:7), God in his righteous vengeance does not pass over him (*Exod.* 12:13). 'Without the shedding of blood there is no forgiveness of sins' (*Heb.* 9:22), and without the forgiveness of sins there is 'a fearful expectation of judgment, and a fury of fire that will consume the adversaries' (*Heb.* 10:27).

Sobering though this may be to contemplate, hell is not empty. There are many there right now, the souls of those who died enemies of God, and they are experiencing the beginnings of their just sentence. Admittedly, the Bible has relatively little to say about hell as a present reality, but it is not completely silent on this subject. Remember Ecclesiastes 12:7: when a man dies 'the dust returns to the earth as it was, and the spirit returns to God who gave it'. In death the spirit of a man returns to God, the Judge of all the earth (*Gen.* 18:25), and it seems reasonable to expect that that must be a judicial encounter, with a just judicial outcome. After all, God does not make believers wait for the beginnings of their just blessedness. Why would he treat unbelievers any differently and put them completely on hold? In the case of the one who dies 'in his sins' (*John* 8:24)—that is, apart from the forgiveness of sins that Christ alone grants—that judicial outcome must be the pronouncing of condemnation and the consigning of the condemned one to the inauguration of the punishment his rebellion long deserved. 'Whoever believes in the Son has eternal life; whoever does not obey the Son shall not see life, but the wrath of God remains on him' (*John* 3:36). For such a one, death must mean crossing over into the realm of God's wrath.

This is confirmed by the story Jesus told of the rich man and the poor man Lazarus (*Luke* 16:19-31), in which both men die, Lazarus entering blessedness but the rich man entering torment; and then a dialogue follows between the rich man and Abraham above. We ought not to press the details of Jesus' story too far, drawing from each and every detail some conclusion about human experience after death. That would be an interpretive mistake. But it is difficult to imagine that Jesus could have told this story if it were not the case that immediately after death unbelievers enter into the beginnings of their everlasting judgment (just as believers enter rest and rejoicing). Otherwise the very structure of the story—not just a detail here or there—turns out to be part reality, part fiction, and Jesus' teaching is evacuated of its impact.

We can go further and say, just as the present inhabitants of heaven are waiting for the last day and all that day will bring, there is waiting in hell too. But there the waiting is so very different from the joyful anticipation that prevails above. In hell the waiting is dreadful. They know the last day will mean their resurrection too: they will receive back their bodies, and thus be fit for their eternal state; they will be made whole again, body and soul reunited. But in their case that wholeness will only make things worse, for it will render them capable of receiving 'whole judgment' in a way they were not before. They will be raised, said Jesus, not unto 'the resurrection of life' but unto 'the resurrection of judgment' (*John* 5:29). On the last day the condemnation of all those who never repented unto God will be publicly pronounced, and then will they be consigned to their everlasting pains. Jesus himself said so. In Matthew 25, referring to the final judgment, Jesus spoke of the two groups into which humanity will be divided: those on his left 'will go away into eternal punishment, but the righteous into eternal life' (*Matt.* 25:46). Eternal punishment, experienced body and soul. This is what those in hell have to look forward to. Their future-looking dread is yet another part of their present pain.

In Chapter 1, as we reflected upon the relationship between the world above (heaven at present) and the world to come (heaven in fullness), I said, 'Heaven is now. Heaven is coming.' Here we have observed that the Bible teaches something similar about hell. Hell is now. Hell is coming. Hell is real.

ETERNAL

The second truth to be affirmed about hell is that hell is *eternal*. This may be the most unsettling aspect of the Bible's teaching on this topic. But let us not shrink back now. Let us not avert our eyes.

In his Second Letter to the Christians in Thessalonica, Paul described the coming day, when the Lord Jesus is revealed from heaven with his mighty angels in flaming fire, inflicting vengeance on those who do not know God and on those who do not obey the gospel of our Lord Jesus. They will suffer the punishment of eternal destruction, away from the presence of the Lord and from the glory of his might (2 *Thess.* 1:7-9).

'Eternal destruction'. Does that mean 'annihilation, obliteration into non-existence', so that hell is not eternal after all? In other words, does Paul mean that the last day (of this present age) will also be the last day of existence for those who remained enemies of God? No, he does not. Given that meaning it would have been purposeless for him to add the adjective 'eternal'. Of course annihilation is eternal: the suggestion that God would annihilate a person and then reconstitute the same person later—'temporary annihilation'—is so silly, so nonsensical, it does not deserve an additional adjective to rule it out. (The same can be said about the Lord's language in Matthew 25 which we noted before: 'eternal punishment'.) As Leon Morris puts it, in this 2 Thessalonians passage: '*Destruction* means not "annihilation" but complete ruin. It is the loss of all that makes life worth living.'[1] This loss, says Paul, this ruin, will never end.

The book of Revelation confirms this interpretation. In chapter 14 an angel describes in chilling terms the judgment that awaits those who side against God and with his unseen opponents and never repent: 'And the smoke of their torment goes up forever and ever, and they have no rest, day or night, these worshippers of the beast and its image, and whoever receives the mark of its name' (*Rev.* 14:11). We read similar language in chapter 20: their destiny is described as 'the lake of fire', and there 'they will be tormented day and night forever and ever' (*Rev.* 20:10, 15).

[1] Leon Morris, *1 and 2 Thessalonians*, rev. ed. (Grand Rapids, Michigan: Eerdmans, 1984), p. 121.

JUST

The third truth to be affirmed about hell is that hell is *just*.

More to the point, we must affirm that God himself—the God who punishes as well as redeems—is just.

This is a vital point to be made close on the heels of our previous one (that is, hell is eternal), because it is precisely the claim that those in hell will suffer forever that strikes many as so *unjust*, if not revolting. Abraham asked God, 'Shall not the Judge of all the earth do what is just?' (*Gen.* 18:25). Many would reply, 'Apparently not. This kind of punishment exacted even for a little while is excessive. This kind of punishment exacted forever makes the God of the Bible a beast, a tyrant, and no just king. In such a God I will never believe.'

The principal problem with this line of thinking and objecting is that its starting place is all wrong. It starts with, 'I have my own notions of right and wrong and the punishment wrong deserves', and from there it eventually reaches, 'I find that the God of the Bible violates my notions.' But the proper starting place is not moral conceptions formed apart from God's truth, by which his Word is subsequently judged and found wanting. This is to move in precisely the wrong direction. Instead we ought to begin with the things that God himself has revealed to be true (both in creation and in Scripture), and then judge our notions by that standard and correct them as needed. I read in Scripture that hell is real, and that hell is eternal. Do I object, 'Unjust! Revolting!'? Then it can only be that I have not begun to grasp the glory of God's infinite holiness and the criminality of man's deep-seated rebellion against him. It must be that I know neither God nor man as I ought. Moses was given just a passing glimpse of the glory of God (*Exod.* 34). Isaiah was given just a brief vision of the holiness of God (*Isa.* 6). Go, interview those two men after such experiences, and ask them if they think eternal punishment meted out to the enemies of God seems excessive or cruel. Not likely. 'The LORD sits enthroned forever; he has established his throne for justice, and he judges the world with righteousness; he judges the peoples with uprightness' (*Psa.* 9:7-8). Let that be our starting point. Let that be our standard, and let our theology rise to it.

And let us be grateful that he is such a God. No one in his right mind would want to live in a world in which the worst of wrongs is left finally unaddressed. No one in his right mind would want there to be a God who reigned in such a neglectful fashion. And what is the worst of all wrongs that might be committed? No, it is not anything we do to one another. Rather, it is the rebellion against our Maker that we instigated in Genesis 3 and have sustained ever since. In heaven and in hell all will finally appreciate just how egregious that rebellion was. Neither in heaven nor in hell, for all eternity, will any more objections to God's justice be heard.

UNSHAKABLE

Hell is real. Hell is eternal. Hell is just.

We have seen that the Bible affirms these three truths. It is worth noting that every human conscience does too. In other words, by these teachings the Bible reiterates what every man already knows deep down. He knows of God's 'invisible attributes, namely, his eternal power and divine nature' (*Rom.* 1:20), which must include God's impeccable justice. Plus he knows 'God's decree that those who practice such things [that is, 'all manner of unrighteousness'] deserve to die' (*Rom.* 1:29-32), a decree left ultimately unfulfilled by anything less than everlasting judgment. This is one of the reasons why turning the pages of the Bible past the 'hell parts' in an effort to avoid that teaching is so futile. Even if you do manage to skip from one uplifting Bible verse to another, deftly avoiding all mentions of wrath and judgment as you hopscotch your way from page to page, carefully selecting passages for your own private promise book, your heart keeps whispering, 'What are you thinking? You bear the image of God. Do you really think you can totally eradicate the justice of God from your own mind and heart? Do you really think you can shrink back altogether from the reality of hell, as if it weren't real after all? Think again.' Yes, many smother that whisper, but it cannot be totally silenced.

This is only reinforced for the Christian by the fact that the Bible's teaching about hell is all bound up with Christ his Saviour. Read the Gospels: Jesus himself spoke often about judgment. Plus, as we saw in 2 Thessalonians, Jesus is the one who will come to judge and destroy (*2 Thess.* 1:7-9). 'The Father judges no one', Jesus said, 'but has given all judgment to the Son . . . And he has given him authority to execute judgment, because he is the Son of Man' (*John* 5:22, 27). Later Christ commanded his apostles accordingly: Peter recorded how the Lord 'commanded us to preach to the people and to testify that he is the one appointed by God to be judge of the living and the dead' (*Acts* 10:42). Shrink back from this doctrine, and you inevitably shrink back from Christ himself: Christ the Teacher, Christ the Judge. Put another way, get to know Jesus and his teachings well, and you will know him as the one who will come on the last day and inaugurate a terrible, unending vindication of justice, as well as finally redeem all his own. Don't go flipping through your Bible looking for some other Jesus than that. You won't find one, not if you read the whole thing.

PROFITABLE

At the outset of this chapter I said the goal was to address the discomfort some Christians feel about hell, discomfort which gets in the way of their rejoicing in heaven. Now that we near the end of the chapter, having reviewed the Bible's teaching, it might be asked, 'So, are we supposed to feel comfortable at this point? Was that the goal? Are we supposed to feel at ease now that we've seen these things?' Well, yes and no.

We should feel comfortable in the sense that we ought to be settled in our minds about the reality of hell, believing firmly what the Bible teaches and harbouring no suspicions that the God of the Bible is unjust. But we should not feel comfortable in the sense that we find these things easy to contemplate, reading Scripture passages about wrath and judgment as if we were reading the sports section in the newspaper. Remember the language of the *Westminster Confession of Faith* which I cited above: even Christians ought to 'tremble at the threatenings' of Scripture. Even those bound for heaven ought to tremble at the thought of hell: not because God might lose us and our destiny change, but simply because hell is so dreadful to contemplate, and many around us are bound for it.

Nowhere do the Scriptures say, 'Set your minds on hell', the way Paul tells us to set our minds on heaven. Nowhere do the Scriptures give us ground to make eternal punishment the most important truth in our theology. But if we wish to do justice to the whole counsel of God, it can hardly be the case that we never pause, even briefly, to consider these things.

Remember Paul's testimony concerning his ministry in Ephesus: 'I did not shrink from declaring to you anything that was profitable' (*Acts* 20:20). Difficult though this may seem, even the Bible's teaching about hell is 'profitable' to us, as all the Scriptures are (*2 Tim.* 3:16). This teaching ought to make a difference in our lives. It should stir a compassionate concern for evangelism, for example, since it impresses upon us the urgency of the gospel. It should stir us to worship too, since it drives us to our knees before the God who is wrathful and whose wrath is just. It should serve as a restraint against sin, as well, since it shows us what sin deserves, and therefore what every sin must be like.

Here is one more difference this teaching ought to make in Christians' lives: it should make us increasingly grateful for the Bible's teaching about heaven. More precisely, it should make us grateful to God that he has made heaven, and not hell, our destiny. 'For God has not destined us for wrath, but to obtain salvation through our Lord Jesus Christ, who died for us so that whether we are awake or asleep we might live with him' (*1 Thess.* 5:9-10). It didn't have to be that way. God didn't have to destine anyone for anything other than wrath. But what did he do? He destined us to obtain salvation, a salvation that amounts to nothing less than living with our Lord Jesus Christ. And live with him we shall, in this life, and then beyond it, and then forever. Christ died for us that it might be so.

So let us not shrink back from the Bible's teaching. God has spoken. 'Let God be true though every one were a liar' (*Rom.* 3:4). Let us believe all that he has said, unsettling truths as well as uplifting. For in this way we lift up our eyes to the God who is, and to no other. Do not shrink back. Do not look away. Instead fix your eyes on him and on the whole of his counsel—for now, perhaps with tears—and you shall never be disappointed.

CHAPTER THIRTEEN

Wayfaring Strangers

We neglect to set our minds on heaven . . .
Because of a failure to grasp our identity in this life as pilgrims on the way.
So let us learn to see ourselves and our lives in that biblical light.

W HEN I was a student at the University of Virginia, I had the privilege of singing in the men's Glee Club. Some people hear 'glee club' and immediately think 'fight songs' or 'show tunes' or 'show choir choreography'. We rarely sang fight songs, we never sang show tunes, and we never, ever did choreography. (For that, our audiences should have been most grateful.) But what we did sing quite often was the Word of God. We did so, not because the Glee Club was founded to sing Scripture and scripturally-themed pieces, but because so many notable choral works in the Western traditions feature such texts, whether passages drawn straight from the Bible or poems based upon its teachings. We took up David's lament over his fallen son, Absalom: 'Would to God I had died for thee, O Absalom, my son, my son' (*David's Lamentation* by William Billings). We confessed with David the virtues of the ideal king: 'He that ruleth over men must be just, ruling in the fear of God' (*The Last Words of David* by Randall Thompson). We wondered with the Psalmist, 'Why do the nations rage?' (*Chichester Psalms* by Leonard Bernstein). We took up the plaintive cry of a downcast soul recorded in Psalm 130: 'Out of the depths I cry to you, O LORD' (*De Profundis* by Arvo Pärt). We surveyed the scene of a devastated Jerusalem using the words of Lamentations: 'How lonely sits the city that was full of people' (*Lamentations of Jeremiah* by Thomas Tallis). And when we performed Handel's *Messiah*—well, we sang the gospel from nearly ever corner of Scripture.

But two pieces we performed that stand out most vividly in my memory were African-American spirituals: 'I Am a Poor Wayfaring Stranger' and 'Soon Ah Will Be Done'. Here are the words:

'I Am a Poor Wayfaring Stranger'

I am a poor wayfaring stranger
While travelling through this world of woe.
Yet there's no sickness, toil nor danger
In that bright world to which I go.
I'm going there to see my father.
I'm going there no more to roam.
I'm only going over Jordan.
I'm only going over home.

I know dark clouds will gather 'round me.
I know my way is rough and steep.
But golden fields lie out before me
Where God's redeemed shall ever sleep.
I'm going there to see my mother.
She said she'd meet me when I come.
I'm only going over Jordan.
I'm only going over home.

'Soon Ah Will Be Done'

Soon ah will be don' a-wid de troubles ob de worl',
de troubles ob de worl',
de troubles ob de worl'.
Soon ah will be don' a-wid de troubles ob de worl',
Goin' home to live wid God.

I wan' to meet my mother.
I wan' to meet my mother.
I wan' to meet my mother.
I'm goin' to live wid God.

No more weepin' an' a wailin'
No more weepin' an' a wailin'
No more weepin' an' a wailin'
I'm goin' to live wid God.

I wan' to meet my Jesus.
I wan' to meet my Jesus.
I wan' to meet my Jesus.
I'm goin' to live wid God.

To this day I can hear those words as they came from our chorus, rising to the high ceilings of the halls in which we performed. Our arrangement of 'Wayfaring Stranger' was slow and mournful. The last word, 'home', we sang in a spirit of quiet contemplation. Our arrangement of 'Soon Ah Will Be Done' was intense and charging. The last word, 'God', we sang as if we wanted to blow the roof off the auditorium to make it easier for the angels to hear us. Nearly twenty years later, I imagine that our resounding 'God' may still be echoing in some of those halls.

Obviously, as a white person born in 1971 who grew up in the comfortable suburbs of Pittsburgh, Pennsylvania, my life-experience was worlds away from that of the men and women who originally created and sang those songs. And yet their words resonated within me, especially during the moments on stage when we were singing them. Those songs touched a spiritual nerve—and the memory of them still does; you might say those words are still echoing in the corners of my soul—because they powerfully captured the spirit of pilgrimage that ought to characterize our Christian experience in this life. At the time I had come to a genuine faith in Jesus Christ only a few years before, and yet even in my relative immaturity as a Christian, and recognizing the simplicity of the poetry, I knew there was something profound about those songs—more profound, in fact, than some of the great choral masterpieces. Here is deep, abiding gospel truth: Christians are pilgrims in this life, and we must learn to see ourselves as such, and live like it. From the Psalms of the Bible to the spirituals of the American experience, the Christian religion has always had its 'pilgrim songs'. All Christians belong to the choir. Consider this chapter a rehearsal. Let us learn well together the songs that God's Word and God's people would teach us.

ON OUR WAY

When we consider what goes into framing a proper pilgrim mentality, three scriptural truths stand out: (1) this world is not our home, (2) heaven is our home, and (3) while we remain here, we are making our way there.

1. This world is not our home.

This comes across in several passages in Peter's First Letter. Indeed, it comes across in the very first verse: Peter greets the Christians of Asia Minor as 'exiles of the dispersion' (1 Pet. 1:1). This sort of language was customarily applied to the Jews as a scattered, away-from-home people, but here Peter uses it to describe the status of the Christian church. He says it again in 1:17: 'conduct yourselves with fear [that is, the fear of God] throughout the time of your exile'. He says it one more time in 2:11: 'I urge you as sojourners and exiles to abstain from the passions of the flesh.' In this world Christians rightly consider themselves exiles, required to live (for a season, not forever) in a setting they cannot call home.

When we say 'this world is not our home', 'world' does not mean planet earth *per se*. After all, in a sense this planet is our home: God made this terrestrial ball to be the habitation of the human race, and the ultimate aim of his redeeming work is not our removal from it but its glorious renewal. Instead, 'world' here means the earth as we find it now, the earth in this 'present evil age' (*Gal.* 1:4). We have in view our planet as the locus of fallen human life with all its sin and misery. Peter is saying, 'You Christians live in such an environment but do not truly belong to it.' We are no longer animated by its rebellion against God. We can no longer identify with its alienation from God. We can no longer relate to its utter hopelessness. Here we feel out of step, out of place. We believe differently. We feel differently. We live differently. For this reason, Peter says, those around us may find our lives somewhat surprising (*1 Pet.* 4:4). Thus we must be ready, he says, to explain ourselves (*1 Pet.* 3:15). What's a hopeful, holy, God-fearing person like you doing in a world like this?

2. Heaven is our home.

If this world is not our home, does that mean we have been left utterly homeless? No, not at all, for heaven is our home. Heaven is the world to which we truly belong, even before our arriving there. Remember our studies in Chapter 2 under the heading 'Our Effectual Calling': the Christian is an already heavenly man; his disposition, desires and justification all belong to the world above; the Christian on earth is 'of heaven but not in it'; heaven is in the believer before the believer is in heaven. As the saying goes, 'Home is where the heart is', and like Paul the Christian's heart longs for the presence of Christ (*Phil.* 1:23), for his 'life is hidden with Christ in God' (*Col.* 3:3). We might even say, 'Home is where the inheritance is', and Peter says to the dispersed exiles of Asia Minor that 'an inheritance that is imperishable, undefiled, and unfading [is] kept in heaven for you' (*1 Pet.* 1:4). In fact, as Jesus said, those two (heart and inheritance) go hand-in-hand: 'For where your treasure is, there your heart will be also' (*Matt.* 6:21).

You see, a world awaits us Christians where we will finally feel at home and at peace. In death we will go there, and then (even more wondrously) at the return of Jesus our heavenly home will come here, for the body will be raised and the cosmos renewed. Finally all will be as it was meant to be. A heavenly earth. Earthly heaven. Then and there we will survey the scene and finally sigh our deepest, most satisfying sigh: 'Home at last!'

3. While we remain here, we are making our way there.

In the meantime, while we remain sojourners and exiles, how are we to occupy ourselves? The answer is, by actively making our way to heaven. With this third truth we round out the idea of pilgrimage. The Bible not only teaches that heaven is our ultimate destination. It also calls us to get up and go there, living a life of intentional heavenward advancement. The Christian life, rightly lived, is marked by a sense of movement, a sense of progress. For example, Paul describes it in terms of walking (*Rom.* 6:4), running (*Gal.* 5:7), and pressing on toward the goal (*Phil.* 3:14). The writer of Hebrews describes it in terms of running 'the race that is set before us', and therefore laying aside every weight which might impede our progress (*Heb.* 12:1). The point is this: our heavenward advancement involves more than the mere passing of time. True, our death and Jesus' return draw nearer in time with the turning of each page on the calendar. But there is more to it than that. Our pilgrimage involves our making the most of the time that is passing: journeying through each day, and then from day to day, and even from year to year, holding fast to Christ and growing in his image. We seek to grow in our love for God and in the fellowship we enjoy with him, which amounts to getting more heaven into our lives now, and thus drawing nearer to our destination. We press on toward the goal, going 'from strength to strength' (*Psa.* 84:7) and from 'one degree of glory to another' (*2 Cor.* 3:18). And with each passing day so lived, 'salvation is nearer to us now than when we first believed' (*Rom.* 13:11).

Of course, this lifelong process of spiritual growth is a journey in a metaphorical sense. After all, throughout the history of the church many Christians have spent their lives growing in Christ this way without ever travelling more than a few miles away from the place where they were born! Whether largely on location or constantly on the move, whether homebodies or frequent flyers, inspired by the Scriptures believers have long understood and described their lives in Christ in terms of pilgrimage, oftentimes doing so in song. This is no 'mere' metaphor, but a mighty one.

In short, we are not just waiting for heaven, but marching there. Putting the two together, we can say that we are wait-marching. (Ah, how useful is the coining of new verbs with a well-placed hyphen!) Behold the Christian as he makes his way, navigating treacherous spiritual terrain, consulting his maps from time to time, swapping stories with fellow travellers, enjoying their company just as they enjoy his, noting the progress he has already made, laying in supplies for the future, contemplating his ultimate destination, and enjoying respites along the way (which is what every Sabbath is meant to be).

Hebrews 11

These three truths we have just considered—(1) this world is not our home, (2) heaven is our home, and (3) while we remain here, we are making our way there—all come together in Hebrews 11. This chapter has been labelled 'The Hall of Fame of Faith'. What makes the faithful men and women of Hebrews 11 deservedly famous? Among other things, this: they knew themselves to be pilgrims, and lived like it:

> These all died in faith, not having received the things promised, but having seen them and greeted them from afar, and having acknowledged that they were strangers and exiles on the earth. For people who speak thus make it clear that they are seeking a homeland. If they had been thinking of that land from which they had gone out, they would have had opportunity to return. But as it is, they desire a better country, that is, a heavenly one. Therefore God is not ashamed to be called their God, for he has prepared for them a city (verses 13-16).

There is the first of our three truths: they 'acknowledged that they were strangers and exiles on the earth'. There is the second: God 'has prepared for them a city'. There is the third: 'they are seeking a homeland'. They are not just waiting for it, but going there. 'They desire a better country, that is, a heavenly one', and the strength of their desire is made manifest in their willingness to make the journey. The writer says, 'these all died' having lived this way. In death were they disappointed? The country they had seen from afar, did it turn out to be a cruel mirage? 'If in Christ we have hope in this life only, we are of all people most to be pitied (*1 Cor.* 15:19). No, in death they found the beginnings of what they were seeking. And at the end of the age they will find the rest of it, and we shall find it with them.

ARE WE THERE YET?

We Christians are heaven-bound pilgrims. The question is, do we see ourselves that way? Have we fostered this kind of pilgrim mentality in our own lives?

If not, impatience may be the culprit. In this respect, many of us have been shaped by our culture more than we care to admit. To put it mildly, our culture is not long on patience. Today conversations are short. Commercials are short. Meals are short. Marriages are short. In short, our collective patience has run short. Even sentences can be cut sh

But the Christian life is long. Yes, as we saw in Chapter 8, it looks short next to eternity, but the Christian life is still long in the sense that it is, literally, 'lifelong', which makes it longer than many other things. It outlasts many careers and relationships and governments and institutions and sports dynasties. Thus understanding the Christian life as a pilgrimage requires us to think and live in terms of a long, arduous journey.

Jonathan Edwards preached a sermon on the Hebrews 11 passage we just looked at. The sermon was entitled 'The Christian Pilgrim, or The True Christian's Life a Journey Towards Heaven'. Edwards said this:

> Long journeys are attended with toil and fatigue, especially if through a wilderness. Persons in such a case expect no other than to suffer hardships and weariness.—So we should travel in this way of holiness, improving our time and strength, to surmount the difficulties and obstacles that are in the way. The land we have to travel through, is a wilderness; there are many mountains, rocks, and rough places that we must go over, and therefore there is a necessity that we should lay out our strength.[1]

[1] Jonathan Edwards, 'The Christian Pilgrim, or The True Christian's Life a Journey Towards Heaven', in *Works of Jonathan Edwards*, vol. 2 (Edinburgh: Banner of Truth, 1995), pp. 243-4.

This is no easy journey. This pilgrimage takes patience. And it is precisely there that we struggle so much.

Children are notorious for pestering their parents from the back seat of the car during long drives. 'Are we there yet? (No.) Are we there yet? (No!) Are we there yet? (NO!)' For the parents this makes the long drive seem even longer. (Of course, when the grandparents hear about this they recognize it for what it is: payback. Years ago, those who are now the tormented were the tormentors. The torch has been passed to a new generation.) The parent who has been asked several times 'Are we there yet?' may reply (calmly, or not so calmly), 'If we were there, we wouldn't still be driving sixty-five miles per hour on the interstate, now would we?' But that reply only has the effect of changing the question to 'Are we almost there? Are we almost there? Are we almost there?' We sinners are an impatient lot.

Sometimes when Christians recite Scripture passages from memory, they succumb to the temptation to recite so quickly they appear to be racing someone else who got a head start. ('I know these words. Let me hurry up and get through them just to prove it.') This is especially ironic when the passage in question is Paul's description of the fruit of the Spirit in Galatians 5. Hurry up and get through it: 'ButthefruitoftheSpiritislovejoypeacepatiencekindnessgoodnessfaithfulnessgentlenessselfcontrol.' 'Wait, go back. Did you say "patience" in there somewhere? Was that in the list?'

One evening after dinner, as my wife and I were cleaning up in the kitchen, one of our children made his way in from the living room and revealed to us that something was troubling him. 'Daddy', he said, 'I don't think we're ever going to get to heaven.' Naturally, my attention quickly turned from drying dishes and wiping countertops to the weighty spiritual concerns of my little one. I gently probed, 'Why do you say that?' He answered, 'Because it's taking so long to get to heaven.'

Priceless!

On the one hand, it was thrilling for me as his father to see that heaven seemed so real to him. I have seen that at other times too, like the time when our children were interrogating their well-travelled babysitter about all the places in the world she had visited, until finally that same son asked with wonder, 'Have you been to heaven?' He knows heaven is real, and he knows it to be the destiny of God's children, even if he did not quite understand at the time all the ins and outs of going there and staying there.

On the other hand, his words in the kitchen that evening struck me as a poignant expression of the impatience that some Christians do feel about going to heaven. We may find it hard to give ourselves wholeheartedly to a difficult journey that may take many years. So instead we settle for an impoverished, 'waiting around' sort of spirituality, and our Christian lives become practically aimless. Instead of pilgrims, we see ourselves as sitters—sitting on a bench, waiting for the bus, and content to nod off until it arrives. Diagnosis: spiritual stagnation.

What is the solution to this plight? How can a pilgrim mentality be nurtured? The solution, in part, lies in grasping the fact that heaven will be worth the wait—or, more fully, worth the wait-march. (There's that helpful hyphen again.) Yes, it will take your whole life to get to heaven, and yes, your life may last longer than most, and yes, the Christian life will be a challenging journey from start to finish. But it's worth it. Not only will heaven itself vastly outweigh the difficulties you knew in getting there, but the life you lived here will have been richer for the sense of pilgrimage you brought to it. You tell me, which is the more satisfying way to spend a day: sitting relatively motionless on a bench, or successfully hiking a challenging climb? Which is the more satisfying way to conceive of your Christian life?

Like all parents, my wife and I have had to teach our children about patience. When they were younger, if they insisted on being served some dish at the dinner table right away, we would sometimes say to them (with deliberate pauses between each syllable), 'You . . . need . . . to . . . be . . . pa- . . . (extra long pause here) . . . tient.' We intended to illustrate by the tempo of our words the very patience to which we were calling them. Does not our heavenly Father train us in a similar way? Think about the tempo of his words. That is, think about the Bible. Think about how the saving purposes of God are gradually, patiently articulated and accomplished from Genesis to Revelation, from protology to eschatology, from Adam to Christ. The Bible is our Father's illustrative way of saying to his children, 'You . . . need . . . to . . . be . . . pa- . . . tient.' Peter reminds us that God himself is patient—'with the Lord one day is as a thousand years, and a thousand years as one day' (*2 Pet.* 3:8)—and he urges us to be patient too.

The good news is, we can be! Patience is named among the fruit of the Spirit. Read Galatians 5:22 (read . . . it . . . slow- . . . ly) and you will see it there. Our Father not only calls us to be patient, but also gives us that gift by the transforming power of his Spirit. 'If we hope for what we do not see, we wait for it with patience' (*Rom.* 8:25). We have the Spirit to thank for that. If you find yourself to be a generally impatient person, and thus reluctant to embrace the identity 'Pilgrim', then return to these truths, and return humbly in prayer to the Spirit whose grace you need. Ask him to help you. Ask him to stir you, so that you rise up from your sitting down and fall in with the hopeful, determined company you see marching by and singing as they go. Christian, your destiny is heaven. Your home is heaven. So get up and go there.

YOUR HEAVENLY LIFE NOW

Thankfully, we pilgrims do not have to wait until we reach heaven to know something of its glories. As we saw in Chapter 11, the church's assemblies for worship afford us foretastes of heavenly experience. And then, even when the worship service ends and we go our separate ways, we continue to enjoy in-breakings of heavenly life now—yes, even in the midst of our sins and sorrows. After all, heaven is a world of love (the theme of another Edwards sermon), as well as a world of joy and peace and holiness and fellowship, and the heaven-bound pilgrim has already begun to experience those realities. Both in his religious exercises and in his earthly callings, insofar as he knows and serves the Lord he has begun to live his future life. The Christian life on earth is life lived in the Holy Spirit (*Rom.* 8:9), and what is heaven but the most Spirit-filled world? Thus our pilgrimage is infused with a sense of the reality of our destination. The way to heaven is by practising heaven. As Edwards put it, 'The way to heaven is a heavenly life; an imitation of those who are in heaven, in their holy enjoyments, loving, adoring, serving, and praising God and the Lamb.'[2]

In the hymn 'Come, We that Love the Lord', Isaac Watts put it this way:

> The men of grace have found
>   Glory begun below;
> Celestial fruits on earthly ground
>   From faith and hope may grow.
>
> The hill of Zion yields
>   A thousand sacred sweets,
> Before we reach the heavenly fields
>   Or walk the golden streets.

[2] Edwards, 'Pilgrim', p. 243.

> Then let our songs abound,
> And ev'ry tear be dry;
> We're marching through Immanuel's ground
> To fairer worlds on high.

In John Bunyan's *Pilgrim's Progress*, Emmanuel's Land was the territory 'within sight of the city', that is, near to the Celestial City, which was the ultimate destination.[3] Watts is saying, that is where we find ourselves now: in sight of the end, not yet having reached it, but marching on until we do. In the meantime we experience foretastes. 'Glory begun below'. Glory before we get there. No, we never sang 'Come, We that Love the Lord' in Glee Club. But Watts' words touch a nerve too, just like the poetry of those two spirituals I mentioned before. Here is a pilgrim song, indeed.

To top it off, this hymn is a pilgrim song that encourages even more singing: 'Then let our songs abound', wrote Watts. Yes, he was right. Let them abound. Think of all the armies throughout history that have sung as they marched. Was there ever a marching people with more cause to sing than the people of Jesus Christ? This world is not our home, but another world is, and we are on our way. No one who spends his life earnestly going there will ever look back and regret it. No one who sings as a pilgrim will ever find that he wasted his breath.

What about you? Think back on recent days and months and years. Have you been sitting, or marching? Better yet, have you been sing-marching? Even as a Christian you may have settled for a relatively sedentary spirituality, but this will not do. Remember, Paul says, 'Set your mind on things that are above' (*Col.* 3:2), and nothing promotes that kind of heavenly-mindedness quite like a deep-seated sense that your whole life is a journey being lived in that direction. So let us live, confident that one day we shall be wayfaring strangers no more. We're only going over Jordan. We're going home to live with God.

[3] John Bunyan, *The Pilgrim's Progress* (Edinburgh: Banner of Truth, 1977), p. 136.

Conclusion:
The Suburbs of Heaven

IN these pages we have covered heavenly ground. We have read our Bibles in order to learn what God says about heaven, and we have also read our own hearts in order to diagnose why we tend not to think about heaven as we should. Some of our reading has been stirring, some of it sobering, but all of it has been designed to fan the flame of heavenly-mindedness in our lives. No doubt there are other factors that cause us to lose sight of heaven in addition to the ones we have considered here. Perhaps this book will spur you to consider what they are and what to do about them. Perhaps heaven will become a topic of conversation in your life, whether around the dinner table or over coffee with fellow Christians, in a way it was not before. I pray the Lord uses this book to bring about such reflection and discussion.

The English Puritan Richard Baxter (1615-1691) was committed to the same cause. In his work *The Saints' Everlasting Rest*, Baxter marshals nearly every argument at hand to persuade Christians to be heavenly-minded. He urges his reader, 'turn thy thoughts from the pursuit of vanity, bend thy soul to study eternity, busy it about the life to come, habituate thyself to such contemplations, and let not those thoughts be seldom and cursory, but bathe thy soul in heaven's delights'.[1] We might wonder, is it worth it to live that way? After all, it takes some effort on our part to 'turn our thoughts' and 'bend our souls' the way Baxter and others urge us. Will those efforts be worth the fruit they bear? Baxter answers, in effect, 'Try it and see. Fill your mind regularly with heaven and see what sort of Christianity it makes.' Baxter writes:

> And when thou hast, in obedience to God, tried this work, got acquainted with it, and kept a guard on thy thoughts till they are accustomed to obey, thou wilt then find thyself in the suburbs of heaven, and that there is, indeed, a sweetness in the work and way of God, and that the life of Christianity is a life of joy.[2]

Fill your mind regularly with heaven, says Baxter, and where will you find yourself? In 'the suburbs of heaven'. That is, you will find yourself in heaven's outlying districts, already beginning to breathe its sweet air and to behold its magnificent skyline, even as you draw ever nearer. Yes, it will be worth it. Try it and see. Set your mind on things above—and keep it there—and life here below will never be the same. May God grant us grace to do so. May he grant us grace to set our sights on heaven.

---

[1] Richard Baxter, *The Saints' Everlasting Rest* (Marshallton, Delaware: The National Foundation for Christian Education, publication date unknown), p. 198.
[2] Baxter, *Saints' Rest*, p. 199.